Jakov Lind

Counting My Steps

an autobiography

Panther

Granada Publishing Limited
Published in 1972 by Panther Books Limited
3 Upper James Street, London W1R 4BP

First published in Great Britain by Jonathan Cape
Limited 1970
Copyright © Jakov Lind 1969
Made and printed in Denmark at
A/S Uniprint, Copenhagen.
Set in Plantin

this book is for my son Simon
and because of Arthur Gregor

To understand the need for history, one must accept Erikson's dictum that "continuity and self-sameness are the prerequisites for an identity." Our instinctual need for procreation and continuity forces us first of all to think continuity. Continuity can be observed only in retrospect. History is the programming of the brain that sets itself at ease by confirming its (the brain's) presence in time - making it, as it were, a reliable guide for future conduct. History is the reassurance the thinking of existence provides itself with. That's why the search for man's origin will continue until he feels no need for identity. Even in the Eastern religions there is a constant reference to the history of its founders. Ergo all existence understood is linear. But its most astounding product, man, "thinks" his own shape as the ultimate form of being.

J.L.

London, December 1968

School for Metaphysics

The world is a maze of bookshops and libraries, editorial offices and universities, studios and stages, stuffed with literature and culture like a rhinoceros with formaldehyde. There is so much good intention in this world, so much belief in reason, friendship, and peace, so much moral outcry, so much printed agony and sheer horror, the best I can do is lock myself in my own mirror of events and see if there is anything left to chew. I can just about recall that fear, real and imaginary fear, is the stuff my life was made of. My roots are fear and fear is in the marrow of my bones. I was brought up to be scared of everything from bread knife to building site. Any vehicle, any electrical appliance, a heavy piece of furniture, and of course any weapon, was called "extremely dangerous". The words hanging, shooting, gassing, etc., were taboo, and of course the word death. At any mention of such a terrible thing the words "God beware" had to be inserted. We were also brought up to fear anyone wearing a cap or a helmet. We were frightened of opulent or obviously rich people and of people with titles or degrees. We might have made fun of someone called Herr Doktor, we knew only too well that a Herr Doktor is no ordinary mortal. Some of this fear explains what happened later.

Fear roots in self-humiliation. To be afraid is to be at someone's mercy. I am afraid means: You are the stronger one. You win. I have nothing left to fear. And it is this kind of fearless courage I needed and still need to face a mirror of things still to come. Being Jewish under the Nazis seems a ridiculously small mishap compared to a nuclear catastrophe that might engulf all of us any day. Meantime we mourn the dead by going on living normally. Indignity and humiliation meted out to all of us who still carry beliefs in reason, friendship and peace, optimism and pessimism, like amulets, are the wages for absolution from guilt. Talking for myself, I rea-

9

lize that my work consists of an attempt to save and change this world with the greatest possible speed and that I will go on saving this world as long as I live. A fossil submerged in shallow water would have an equal chance. All that's left to do is to tell what happened. Counting my steps from one tree to the next, the forest of infinite madness is, at least, terminated by a real space and a real time.

A few months ago I had a vision of a stream of life engulfing the earth—it looked like millions of naked humans being vomited up from a crater, flying through the air and hitting the ground like locusts — no, like people. It was just like the opening of Dante's Hell. The dead returned to the living. Or maybe it was like the Day of Judgement and all who ever died, the millions of generations of men became alive again, and presumably went home to have another meal. I saw a crater spewing out mankind, covering the earth with "human beings". First I thought I had seen the beginning of the world, later I presumed I must have seen the end of all days. On reflection I realize: That is exactly what is going on now, right now, this hour. So how can one really be concerned with either past or future if it happens now?

The attic of my nineteenth-century soul is stuffed with weird obsessions. Future, past, hope, justice, Socialism to name but a few. The things in my attic were once Everything. And Everything has its place, a few places in fact. The main entrance to this School for Metaphysics had high wrought-iron gates and spiky grilles and led into a gravelled forecourt with old chestnut trees. A red tiled roof covered Everything solidly planted in shifting Danube mud, a white flagpole grew out of a yellow wall made transparent by huge Gothic windows. The place called itself in red letters: *PRIMARY SCHOOL FOR BOYS OF THE CITY OF VIENNA*, Schüttaustrasse. We lived across the road in a new workers' housing estate called the Goethehof, another wing of esoteric instruction, cramped with strangely familiar junk.

Ferdinand Hartl, fat, dark, pink-cheeked, unfolded a clean handkerchief to make sure that there were no rabbits inside. He pointed to the centre of the clean handkerchief and explained: "This we call the centre of the handkerchief. We call it the centre because it's in the middle. Everything that's in the

10

middle we call the centre. The centre looks like a cross. Can everyone see the cross?" I thought that this is not required learning for a Jewish child, but being the first day at school I did what the others did, I stared at the point Hartl indicated. "Well, how do we use a handkerchief? We don't use it like that" — he pretended to clean his nose on the end of the linen — "no, that would be wrong and wasteful. We use it like this: first we clean our nose in the centre and then we continue this action clockwise, only if necessary of course, round and round, making the circle. Here the circle gets bigger and bigger and now when we reach the edge of the handkerchief, what do we say?"

We were too shy and baffled to attempt an answer. "Well if not one of the children knows, I will tell you. We say: Now the handkerchief is full. Finished." We all nodded approval. "What do we call it?" And forty-two boys shouted as loud as they possibly could: "Full and finished." "Yes," Hartl continued, "the handkerchief is now full. But we don't throw it away (We shouted, "No."); we don't wipe our face with it (We yelled, "No."); we don't put it in our pocket and keep it there for a few days (There was no shouting of approval, because it seemed not to be very logical.); no, we give it to our mother and say: 'Here mother, my handkerchief is full. May I please have a clean one?' Well, what do we say, when the handkerchief is full and we give it to our mother?" "Here mother, my handkerchief is full. May I please have a clean one?" We shouted as loudly as possible and were so pleased with the obviously correct solution to a serious problem, we started to clap, whistle, and shout even more.

That was lesson number one. Lesson number two was religious instruction, not obligatory for Jewish children, fascinating all the same. Father Kirchner, a slim, young man in long black skirts, showed us the beginning of the world in coloured chalks on a blackboard. Adam and Eve and the snake and the apple in Paradise. A very exciting view of post-mortal location. The lesson opened and finished with "Our Father which art in Heaven ..." I didn't have to learn the words. I couldn't speak them out loud. The father might have found out that Catholic was not my religion and I would have been embarrassed. I learnt that there is a Paradise and was promised a view of hell within a week, besides being taught how to keep my nose clean at all times. A good beginning. I think that after this first day I must have decided to block my ears with the forefinger of each hand for the next few years and all future, because to listen to what Hartl (the Trottel) had to say was admitting to ignorance and stupidity. When it came to maths, for instance, Hartl wanted to know how much 23 and 31 could possibly be. As if he didn't know it himself. Even if I knew the right answer (adding and subtracting were easy) it was beyond my dignity to admit it. Only children who would one day inherit a grocery store should take note of such trifles. I would never own a grocery store, because a grocery store had once upon a time, before the first war, been in the family. Butter and salami were bought on credit. I knew I was never going to sele them. Why keep groceries unless you want to eat them? The good old times had turned sour like fresh cream, without the preserving icebox of the Monarchy. Emperor Franz Josef was buried under shelves full of sardines and salmon, his nephew Emperor Karl lay under the apples and oranges. A rotten lot, the Habsburg specialities.

Maths were learned in life. In life there was more than adding and subtracting. There was also: to count with, to settle, to figure out, and to take into account. To calculate how to live with less than a hundred schillings a month was a practical problem solved only by adding small amounts temporarily held in trust for us by neighbours and relatives. As others kept our money in their pockets, an occasional reminder — "Please lend us forty or sixty schillings" — was useful. We didn't count on miracles, though we were always ready for them. If the Messiah had entered the Goethehof on his white donkey we would have been among the first to be downstairs. As it was, we counted on help and got it. We might have eaten a bit less but were not starved. Weaker people might have been undernourished with our diet; we, probably descending from Giants, were made "of iron". Sometimes one heard it said: "Look at Frau Lederer, she looks so healthy, is there nothing wrong with her?" There was certainly nothing wrong with our health. "Health is the main thing," they said at home.

More interesting but not less difficult than figuring out how to live was writing. To learn to say A B C D E was easy, to put the letters together so as to make words out of them, highly complicated. No doubt, without my special talent for writing, I would never have succeeded in writing down:

12

"Rudi and Mimi are asleep. In the window a shoe and another shoe." While my sisters wrote: "Rudi and Mimi are asleep in the window. A shoe and another shoe," I knew straight away that Rudi and Mimi had their shoes in the window to find them stocked full with sweets on Saint Nicolaus day.

More difficult than copying was spelling. A single word had sometimes one and sometimes two syllables. To know when to break up a word and when to rejoin it was magic. Why some words had one and others two of the same letter, no one could explain. Why not sistter if you felt like saying sistter? I could annoy my eldest sister in particular by writing her with two t's. But Hartl said: "No, sister with one t." No point in explaining: "Sir, my sister, you don't know her, she hits me whenever she can." I wanted to write sister with two t's and child with one, house with two s's and schwarz like schwartz. But the rule wouldn't allow it. The rule was made by Hartl and Hartl was always right. He was a dictator. In 1938, one of the first to wear a big swastika in his buttonhole, it didn't surprise me. Hartl was equally pedantic on the problem of ink stains. Children were not allowed to have a dripping or breaking pen. Every child with more than one spot on a page had to tear up the page and start all over again; you had to be lucky to make your spot after the first word and not after the one before last. Writing had to be *neat* and *correct*. The punishment was a dreaded number four, if not an eternal repetition of the same sentence over three pages.

With a certain strength of character I defended myself against writing for a long time. I hated to write because I hated the rules against spilling of ink. Spots, dots and lines, doodles and drawings, everything done with black ink on white paper was writing to me. My parents were on Hartl's side, they agreed with this old Nazi that lines and dots are permitted only if made to look like words. Yet words looked to me like unimaginative drawings. They still look the same to me now. We read words *because* we think they are inportant, *because* we presume that by reading words we understand the mind. A kind of perfect insanity. I *never* understood what I read, *never* understand what I write, and cannot understand how other people may presume that they understand what they read and write. How can the picture in front of one's eyes be drawn with words? How can the intellect reflect itself in letters? Figures are useful for trade and the

13

calculation of time and distance. To write words is a ridiculous waste of ink on paper, to read words is madness. Once I had learnt to write "Elfi and Heini walk in the park" I saw no reason why I should be made to read this sentence as well. To read what one had written down? Why read what you already know? After all, I had written the sentence *myself* — and to read what one had *not* written oneself seemed even more insane. Why should a stranger be made to go through such torture? I decided that I would never read, never. Either I will write or read. But certainly not both.

Not only were we forced to read: we had to read everything out loud. "Sir, I have read this already, I know what's in it." Hartl: "How do I know that you know?" I: "Because I know that I know and that's enough." "No nonsense, Lind, who the hell do you think you are? If you don't read it out loud, I can't know whether you know." I read out loud: "a bag, a house, a tree, a man," with the *right* pronunciation on vowels and consonants. That's how children lose their innocence. By forcing them out of their silence into the noisy world of the written and spoken word; instead of *knowing* we were taught to *understand,* instead of *feeling* we were taught to *talk.* Thank God.

Hartl, who forced me to read and write, taught me to read my mother's poems and to copy them. My mother kept several notebooks of her poems (in ink and pencil) under the sheets in the linen cupboard. We were allowed to read them, providing we put them back in their place, under the linen with lavender and mothballs. Hartl taught me to read poems that rhymed with red and death, on life and tears. Hartl taught me in essence to understand the finer things of this world turning yellow under the mothballs. Nearly all of life was condensed to tears and pains my mother described, echoing what she had learnt from Goethe and Schiller and a few lesser lights of German fogginess. As soon as I could copy these poems, without anyone noticing that I had done just that, I did of course. I didn't like to wear my mother's clothes but I liked to be able to write poems just like her and if possible better. Her poems were not "strong"; they were soft and full of pity for the ill and the dying. The ill and the dying were the sloppy kind of people. I preferred the soldiers in uniform on picture postcards sent from the front and kept in shoe cartons. The whole family in Austrian uniform. This is your Uncle Hein-

14

rich and this your Uncle Solomon and this is your father and this a cousin of his sister-in-law. I probably wanted to be a soldier. My mother wrote like a "civilian". No recommendation. Platitudes in the cupboard and a repetition of irrelevancies at school. Where was the truth? The truth was in books. To know books meant knowing authors and titles and if possible some of the contents. But mainly authors and titles. As there were tramps and great men in the ordinary world there were good and bad books in the world of letters. Novels were better than science books, science better than adventure, adventure considered more classy than funny books, and funnies much better than crime stories; but even crime stories were better reading than newspapers. The lowest rag was still considered higher literature than a prayer book. AUTHORS WERE GODS. ALL OF THEM. Heinrich Heine, the converted German Jew, Friedrich Rückert, and Hoffmann von Fallersleben. Everything they wrote cleverly managed to rhyme with death and heart. Wilhelm Busch and his *Max and Moritz*, Erich Kästner of *Emil and the Detectives*, Ringelnatz, Christian Morgenstern were the funny men. Goethe and Schiller one only knew by heart. Whatever they had written was holy.

Names, names, we had to collect names. Chaim Nachman Bialik, but I don't know what he wrote; Beer-Hoffman I can still recite. Those were "our" poets. Franz Werfel *(Der Stern der Ungeborenen,* a novel that takes place in 3000 A.D., and *The Song of Bernadette)* was a big writer, no doubt, or we wouldn't have bothered with him. Jakob Wassermann of *Das Gänseblümchen,* I don't know why I loved it so much. We called him "worthwhile". Hans Fallada: *Wer einmal aus dem Blechnapf frass* described the working-class districts. Cabbage smells in dark backyards. Children living on crime. Kollwitz, Liebermann, and Zelle might have provided the illustrations. Fallada was Berlin. Emile Zola, a "decent" man, obviously not an Austrian, had something to do with the trial of Captain Dreyfus. He wrote *J'Accuse,* accusing the accusers of Captain Dreyfus of anti-Semitic prejudice. Zola's *Nana,* about a prostitute called Nana, was under-the-counter reading, very sexy; his *Germinal,* a moving tale about the misery of miners in the north of France. You could get away with not having read *Nana* or *Germinal,* but anyone who had to admit that he knew nothing of *The Brothers Karamazov, The*

Idiot, or *The Insulted and Injured* might as well have left town. Dostoyevsky was "difficult"; he had many, too many, characters in his books, but all of them interesting, passionate people and even the murderer Raskolnikof was an exceedingly "human" being, not scum. Dostoyevsky was our writer. He and Gorky. Maxim Gorky talked about proletarians and their misery as Dostoyevsky talked about generals, rich businessmen, beautiful and heartbroken women, and innumerable, wretched aristocrats. Dostoyevsky and Gorky explained the world around us. Vienna, too, was full of impoverished and unhappy aristocrats, petit bourgeoisie, starving workers, and crazy *Luftmenschen.* But Viennese writers seemed not to write about them. Stefan Zweig wrote about characters with human weaknesses and dark passions, usually noble, elegant, and a little melancholic. Schnitzler had plenty of artists *manqué,* doctors who had loused up their careers because of some stupid love affair with an actress. His Austrian officers were highly sexed and running up debts, shooting themselves if they couldn't settle them on demand. Feuchtwanger and Wassermann, Arnold Zweig and Thomas Mann wrote about unhappy people who suffered and cried, but none of them ever suffered as deeply as the Russians of Dostoyevsky and Gorky. I never read *War and Peace* at that time, but I had read *The Kreutzer Sonata* and *Anna Karenina,* and I still believe that every lonely woman on a forlorn railway platform is ready to throw herself under a train. When Russians made a mess of their lives, it seemed to be a real mess; when Germans and Austrians did the same it somehow never seemed to be final. I preferred Russian resignation to hopelessness, to the twisted German notions of hope. The Russians were funnier too. Gogol's Revisor was not only a scoundrel, he was a lovable man as well. Nestroy's Lumpacivagabundus a mere clown compared to him. Besides: Gogol looked like a real writer, so did Dostoyevsky, Gorky, Tolstoy. They all had beards or moustaches or long hair. German writers looked like businessmen or bank clerks. Take Thomas Mann. *Buddenbrooks* seemed never to end and the author was a clean-shaven Herr Doktor. Compare Turgenev's looks to the looks of Rilke! What a difference! The Russians were romantic and tragic, the Germans confused and pitiful. But we liked Rilke. Rilke was both romantic *and* genuinely sad. The early death of the Cornet convinced me that there was no heroism in being a soldier. Rilke lamented the death of a young soldier, Erich Maria Remarque cursed the war. *All Quiet on the Western Front* taught me at the age of nine that war is shit, lice, mud, a trench full of foul-smelling bodies, gouged-out eyes, and torn-off limbs, the ordinary soldier digging his grave while officers are having a great time in the casinos and brothels. I loved uniforms and arms, and above all, the flags, the sashes, and the medals of the Army. But I hated war. All the writers I knew hated war. Tucholsky, Bertolt Brecht, Arnold and Stefan Zweig, Romain Rolland. Everyone in fact. They hated war and they hated the rich and the powerful, the aristocrats, the bankers, the factory owners, exploiters of the people. This was a lousy, stupid, depraved world, clearly visible, and by reading about it we "understood" why it was so. There was no escaping from the truth. A few apologists tried. Hermann Narziss for instance. In *Demian* and *Steppenwolf, Narziss und Goldmund,* Hesse, so it seemed, tried to apologize for "general human failures"; life, he made you feel, is a labyrinth populated by passionate, torn-in-half souls. To Rabindranath Tagore it didn't even matter if you were alive or dead. One big cosmic circle. To his Buddha birth and death are the same thing. We didn't like that, we rejected this soft-pedalling. We wanted to hear "Yes" or "No", "Forward" or "Backward", something about a golden future or a dark past. The children of the first Austrian Socialist Republic knew right from wrong straight away, providing they would read.

Have you read Hesse?

Yes, of course.

Did you like him?

I liked him.

He is good, yes?

Yes, very good.

What did you read?

I forgot.

Liar. Have you read Tolstoy?

Who?

Tolstoy.

Tolstoy, Tolstoy. Of course I have read Tolstoy.

Don't tell me you don't know Tolstoy either?

Who?

I can tell you are a damned liar. He hasn't ever read Tolstoy!

I read him, of course I did.

What did he write?

What did he write?

War and Peace, you idiot.

Oh, this Tolstoy. Why didn't you say so. Of course I read *War and Peace*. I didn't know what, what's his name, wrote it.

What is it about?

Napoleon.

Someone must have told you that. Who wrote *Romain Rolland?*

Romain Rolland, Romain Rolland ...

Don't stutter.

Romain Rolland is by Stefan Zweig. I should have known.

By Stefan Zweig? What else is by Stefan Zweig? Is Arnold Zweig his brother? Did Werfel write *Buddenbrooks* or was it Thomas Mann? And what else did Werfel write?

Wait a minute, wait a minute.

What's wrong with you? Don't you read?

Yes I read.

Well, then remember. *The Hunchback of Notre Dame* is by Wassermann.

Are you sure?

As sure as you have lost your brains.

But who wrote *Sergeant Grischa?*

Who cares? *Sergeant Grischa* was written by Sienkiewicz.

I thought Sienkewicz wrote *Quo Vadis.*

Never, you fool. *Quo Vadis* was written by Rilke.

I don't believe you. I'll ask my mother.

Run and ask her. She doesn't know.

Which was usually the truth. But my mother owned Heine and Goethe, which set us miles above the other children; in fact I felt so far above the other children that I was, a lot of the time, alone.

My brain remains stuffed with old bicycles, with rubber hoses and moth-eaten mattresses, with dusty, torn lampshades and half-dismantled stoves. I think wrecked baby prams without wheels. My ears are full of broken glass and my throat is crammed with marbles. Whoever needed all that, will anyone

18

ever make use of it again? Nothing was ever thrown away. You never know, it could come in handy ... one day.

One day, from the moment the Messiah blows his trumpet, the Swiss and the Swedes will rise from their graves, fresh, clean, and diligent as ever. A second blast of the trumpet and the Swiss will carry on where they left off: to make the Kingdom of the Lord come true right here in our world. A ventilated, sterilized locker for eternity will be this world if the Swiss and the Swedes pull off a Second Coming. And for all I know they might succeed. A brave new world lies at the far end of this Swiss lake, so dull and uniform, we'll hardly notice it. The good old times of 1984, when there was still excitement, the good old times when they still bothered to reform the individual's mind, the golden age of brainwashing, the grandchildren of my grandchildren will say. I will not be among them, as I am not with them now. If I'm sick I vomit broken china and golden frames. What, if not handmade in the nineteenth century, is my Middle European soul? And not just a common soul, a better-than-average soul. The better people of the Prater were freshly shaven and wore ordinary businessmen's suits. Better people (Jewish, of course) are not only better compared to non-Jews, which they are anyway, each better person had to feel himself better than another. To prove his point he ought to despise his neighbour. I am the third child of such a family of better people. Our philosophy was simple, our logic brilliant. "Better is what thinks itself better. If you don't believe it, no one else will." Whether others believed us or not, we were probably the best of all people. We didn't think much of our neighbours and friends. The advantages of belonging to the better people are obvious: once you feel better anyway, you are not concerned with the obvious exhibits of human quality, like beautiful clothes, furniture, or cars. The drawbacks are not minimal. A child of a better family is not allowed to whistle, spit, shout, or piss in the street. A better person one cannot become; one just is or is not. For us impoverished gentry of castles in the clouds, everything but the lack of money was fun. Or nearly everything. Being Jewish was not always fun either. But sex, religion, politics, literature, life and death were fun. One could make a joke out of everything, even about being Jewish and being without money, but "a joke is a joke". Deep down we knew

19

better: a poor man does not count, a poor Jew has no justification to call himself alive. Too many poor Jews in Vienna, too many poor people in general. As soon as I opened my eyes I learnt to inspect cut, colour, and quality of everyone's dress. THE DRESS IS THE MAN should be a good slogan in neon lights. It was one of the first of a long row of "truths" instead. The dress is the man? Not too hard to pick this truism to bits. How about: A POOR MAN DOES NOT COUNT? Harder to disprove this dogma. Our clothes were in reasonably good shape (patches counted as "honest", dirt as vile) but we definitely did not count in any court. The first time a child in the street, or was it at school, called me "dirty Jew" I knew he had a point there. Though we were not really dirty, the house wasn't always tidy. My mother had no money, four children, and no help in a three-room flat. I couldn't apologize for her, that's where all the later trouble began. Not only might we have been untidy and maybe a little bit dirty in the corners and under the carpet, "Dirty Jew!" was no joke, it was a crime with a suspended death sentence.

For many years I regarded this period as something shameful and ridiculous, like a crooked small toe or a wart on a finger, at other times as the days of glorious heroism. How did we ever survive poverty, humiliation, and the anti-Semitism of neighbours and schoolmates? At times I saw ourselves as martyrs putting up a last fight in the sewers of a ghetto we never lived in. Only recently the picture changed: Vienna was probably a suburb with chimney pots on impressive, old, large buildings, reeking in the waste waters of the several Danubes and the town was somewhere else. The town was Paris, London, or New York. From New York came the suits and dresses of silk, crumpled and smelling of mothballs, but pure silk! White shoes with perforated heart-shaped tops, underwear that was slit from behind and ties and women's hats in many colours, white gloves and white socks (What can you do? They like white over there!), my mother bundled and sold it all to Meyer, Vienna's biggest dealer in secondhand clothes. Because: "Who can wear these rags?" Maybe for a week or two, just for fun, we would keep a pair of white gloves and play Americans, with dark glasses and hats on. (Who could have mistaken one for anything else?) In the end America was more useful to Meyer than to us. My mother wrote letters of thanks, claiming that every single item was a most valuable addition to our wardrobe. But not only did the discarded presents not fit anyone, we would have been embarrassed and ashamed to wear any of these alien, exotic garments. Everybody would notice straightaway that the clothes were not new. Mended clothes were nothing to be ashamed of, but secondhand clothes? Secondhand clothes were for the tramps and the really poor. We considered ourselves temporarily out of money (because of the Wall Street crash, etc., etc.) but never poor. We don't need their pity, it was said. Better people are proud. We felt sorry for pregnant unmarried women, insane criminals, rich relatives. What's the point of having "just money" and nothing else? A rich man who had "nothing but money" is poor, that's how we learnt it from my mother. A future genetic incubator will no doubt be able to manufacture better people. Here are the ingredients: a father who loves operettas and a mother who prefers books. A father who spends his days in the coffeehouse, or somewhere else — a mother who sits at home with the children. A better person is obviously something very complicated.

At the very base of the pyramid of people, still half covered in mud, started the peasant and we never considered him to be human at all. The peasant was a species all by himself. Alien like Indians and Abyssinians. There were friendly peasants and nasty peasants, generous peasants and greedy peasants. But peasants. To quote: *"Ein Bauer ist kein Mensch"* (A peasant is not a human being).

The human ladder, so it was generally assumed, didn't start until halfway up anyway. It started with the fellowman; underneath the fellowmen crawled all kinds of creatures, the UNTERMENSCHEN (subhumans) were Jews and communists; VIECHER (beasts) were murderers, rapists, and dangerous sex-killers; UNGEZIEFER (insects) usually referred to Jews and Poles; DRECK (dirt) could only be Jews, poor Christians, and Serbians; GESINDEL (scum) were the beggars, petty thieves, gypsies, and Jews; SCHWEINE (pigs) were Jews *and* Nazis; MIST (dung) inferior midgets, idiots, prostitutes, and pimps.

The first human was the fellowman (*Der Mitmensch*). The fellowman is a friendly neighbour, a harmless passenger on the streetcar, a blind old woman. A "Person" or an "Indivi-

21

duum" were not necessarily human. "This person" was a bitchy housewife, a nonpaying subtenant; "this Individuum"— a murderer and rapist. "A human being" (*der Mensch*) could only support his claim with the help of an adjective. A fine man, a nice man, a cordial man, a courageous man, a funny man. Broll, f.i., was a fine man, one could borrow money from him; a good man was Silber, one couldn't borrow anything from him but he listened patiently to other people's misery; a nice man was Mittler looking after his big family; a cordial man was Wedeles — greets you before you greet him; a courageous man was Fürst — dying of cancer and breathing to no one a word; Oswald the tailor, twenty warts on his face, poor and with a sick wife, was neither human nor anything else. But even Oswald could have been a "better person" had he hidden his misfortunes better. The *Mittelmensch* (in-between man) was by the classic definition neither a great light nor a small fool. Acquaintances, teachers, businessmen, small manufacturers and the parents of our friends were *Mittelmenschen*.

Above man stood superman. An *bermensch* lives a lonely life amidst his old German furniture. Einstein, Freud, Theodor Herzl, Hesse, and Dostoyevsky. Superman and genius were more or less the same. There were not too many of them and everyone knew them from books and posters. Nietzsche, Wagner, Schweitzer, Max Reinhardt, all of them *bermenschen*.

Is Einstein a genius?

Well, of course.

Is Karl Lueger a genius?

Don't ask so stupid.

Is he a genius or is he not a genius?

Of course he is not a genius.

Why not?

He hasn't invented anything. (A genius had to be world-famous *and* a good man.)

Is Madame Curie a genius?

Are you crazy? How can she be a genius?

But she invented something.

But she is not a genius — she is just a great person.

A great person was not necessarily world-famous and rich and good. Ferdinand Lassalle, f.i., was such a great person; and a great person (but not a great man) was Vienna's Mayor

Karl Seitz; a great man was Zola (and, some people claimed, a genius). Achad Haam, Ben-Gurion, Aron David Gordon. Great People.

On the very top of the pyramid sat the heroes: Bar Kokba, Judas Maccabaeus, Prince Eugene, Max Baer, world heavyweight champion, Michael Stroganoff, *The Courier of the Czar* (a famous movie), Karl May, Attila the Hun, Lord Byron, Richard the Lionhearted. Dollfuss was called "a fine hero", which was no longer a compliment.

Above the heroes high up in the sky floated the poets: Goethe, Schiller, Heine, Nestroy, and two dozen others. And above all the great men in the world next to God sat the greatest of them all — my father, Simon, looking out of the window and puffing clouds of smoke. A man simultaneously proud and ashamed. Proud because he refused to behave like a poor and unsuccessful businessman and ashamed because he was just that. When he left his window he travelled with samples of linen and worsted to show them to anyone who cared to look. He claimed to be selling underwear to nuns. Occasionally he came home for a haircut, a change of laundry, with a suitcase full of toys. When he came home the flowers on the kitchen wall shone in summer splendour, when he left they wilted and could be swept up from the red linoleum. It was better to have a father on the road than no father at all. As soon as he was gone, we chalked it up at the local delicatessen, hoping for a war or disaster to wipe out the debts.

Luftmensch was a Viennese businessman without much business in the world. Half *Luftmesch* and half duke. He gave generously and borrowed heavily. He always wore a grey suit and a red tie, his collar and cuffs were specially hand-laundered and starched at the Habsburg Steam Laundry. His moustache was of tobacco colour, a small, brown brush underneath a fleshy but straight nose. He was not tall, but not small either, and heavy-set. He had a bald head, occasionally ringed by hair. If he didn't wear galoshes he wore brown *Gamaschen* over his high laced boots. He always wore a waistcoat and his watch on a golden chain if he hadn't pawned it. In all his pockets he had cigarettes like others carry small change, and smoked twenty more cigarettes and whistled well-known tunes from operettas. He held a cup of coffee like a countess, the small finger of his right hand slightly bent, because of a bullet that had gone right through his palm on the Galician Front a year before the armistice. The government owed him a living. He was a 35 percent war invalid; had he lost the entire hand the government would have granted him the special licence to sell cigarettes and tobacco in a Tabak-Trafik.

My father spoke to no one in particular but a great deal to himself. He had friends but not one friend: he had friends for the coffeehouse, friends to play cards and dominoes with, friends to hatch out deals with, with the help of a scrap of paper and a small stump of pencil. His friends were called Feuerstein and Auerbach, Morgenstern and Wedeles. They were skeptical and funny, apolitical and a-religious, they made jokes and played dominoes, they loved to watch women from behind their newspapers and talk politics and the "market". They all smuggled foreign exchange, were always evading taxes and in debt to everyone. Hippies in galoshes.

I try to find some special virtues in my father and all I can remember are his generosity and unusual good humour. He gave "last suits" away to poor men at the door and joked about the religious who shouted at God ("a feeble, fragile old man") to give them more and more money. My father loathed the Orthodox Jews. He despised the righteous and the respectable, called them "all hypocrites".

He was born in Rabka in the Zakopane on the Polish side of the Tatra Mountains, an hour's drive from the Czech border. A real Austrian. Vienna was, even in his time, not more than six hours by train. He was the youngest of five brothers. His brothers were called Ignatz, Adolf, Hermann, and Heinrich. He had a sister a few years younger called Augusta. Gusti for short. My father's father, Jakob, died when my father was two. All we knew about his mother was her name. She was called Maria Silberring and God knows what kind of woman she was. We never saw a picture of either of them. Rabka still is a *Kurort,* a place high up in the Tatra, a place to which people from Cracow and Warsaw come by train for summer hikes and winter sports or to dry out their lungs in one of the many sanatoria. No *stettel* this Rabka, no ghetto. Just an ordinary small provincial town living off its tourists and sufferers of consumption. Either his brother Ignatz or Adolf had the restaurant licence at the railway station. Father Jakob left a general store and some farmland when he died but should have shared it out himself. When the brothers did there was nothing left for the youngest one.

He left home at the age of eleven to learn the textile trade in Budapest or Vienna. It must have been 1895. In 1904, long before the big stream of war refugees arrived from the East, he was already "an old Viennese" and not a little proud of that. Sometime between 1905 and 1915 he ran or owned with his sister a delicatessen in the third district, but after the war, when they discharged him from the Army, he somehow had lost every share in it. He went into spray guns. Spray guns to pump fresh air into cinemas. Whether he manufactured them or bought the stocks from a factory I don't know; in any case he had salesmen travelling for him who disappeared with order books, samples, addresses, and cash before he realized what was going on.

He went into business with his brother Heinrich, into textiles. They had a shop or an office in the ninth district. Heinrich was tall, had the same colour and shape moustache (a Hitler-Chaplin moustache) and not a hair on his head either. I always thought the two brothers must have been redheaded when younger, but I'm told except for the moustache their hair was pitch black. They didn't look Jewish, they looked Viennese. My father was neither as tall as his brother Heinrich, nor was he as tough and shrewd. When Heinrich won, Simon (my father) lost. When Heinrich still had a car left, my father used public transport and looked like he didn't care. It made no difference to him. He didn't care about money, he didn't care about the Jewish religion, he seemed not to care too much about the family, what did he care for? He could tell whether it was wool or cotton by burning a single thread and sniffing at it, but I'm sure he didn't care about this bit of professionalism either. He probably cared about women. We have no proof. He was an ordinary father, an ordinary Viennese, as an ordinary Viennese he felt better than all the other ordinary Viennese. I loved my father and my "fatherland". Even now, after thirty years, when I curse or ridicule Vienna and the Viennese at the slightest provocation, I know I am in love with the town. I'm in love with my hatred.

The roots of the Middle European are in the landscape. We are landlocked people with our love-hatred for the town of our birth. Unlike people born on the coasts of the Continent

25

who occasionally sensed a breeze from other worlds with fresh, new ideas, we seemed to walk the treadmill of the oldest empire on the Continent, partly in circles under the weight of Teutonic, Slavic-Jewish ideals, partly we lay between the millstones and were ground to fine powder for the keg of utopian anarchistic revolutions. The fact is: my father was Austrian to the core. That he was born in Poland and a Jew made him just that bit more of an Austrian. Austria and especially Vienna was not just a town, it was a philosophy of mutual tolerance of the most varied kind of people. Not a program but a way of life, an easygoing way of life. The crux of the matter is: Jews will always feel European above everything else; Europe has been the fatherland for two millennia and Israel today is a state modelled after the Austrian Empire as New York is the most European town outside Europe. Most Jews had a chronic financial problem on the Continent which became acute in the thirties and above all in Vienna. Fathers had to provide.

My mother was called the Saint. The Good One. The Strong One. The Patient One. She was of medium height, round, blue-eyed, brown hair, a turned-up nose, high cheekbones; she looked Russian and had strong and very skilful and elegant fingers. She was from a good family, from decent stock, and had innumerable uncles, aunts, and cousins in town to testify to this. How my father must have loathed her family who always took her side. In the eyes of her family he was always irresponsible, easygoing, too generous, unreliable, etc. He wasn't successful and only murder or conversion were greater sins. Her father, Mechel Leib Birnbaum, had been a pillar of the Snyatin Jewish community and a well-to-do cattle dealer from Snyatin on the Pruth, between Kolomea and Czernowitz, was not a nobody. His wife, Ethel, reportedly made the rounds of the poor and orphans with pots of homemade chicken soup. The Birnbaums were respectability, decency, and honesty incarnate, besides being "cultured". My mother could recite Goethe and Heine, she had learnt it in their German school. Even if my father had known who Goethe and Heine were (and he must have known that from hearsay),he would never have told a soul. A professor,he once said, is a man who is not clever enough to be something else.

How the Birnbaums and my father met? With the help of a marriage broker I am told. There was nothing wrong in consulting a marriage broker at this "late age in life". He was about thirty-five and still a bachelor and she was twenty-seven and a refugee. She came to Vienna when the Cossacks moved toward Snyatin. Before marriage she had done all kinds of jobs. Learnt cutting and sewing, had worked at one of the big Delka shoe stores, managed by her Uncle Karl. Her brothers were married, her mother dead, her father an old man; what should she do in Snyatin again? Keep house for Mechel Leib? The family was mobilized and somehow they found the best possible party. The distant relative Simon L.

She probably was a virgin of twenty-seven and he a man of the world. Maybe they even fell in love. Grandfather Mechel Leib with deep-set blue, honest eyes, must have seen a playboy in this young assimilated man, who knew nothing of Torah and Talmud. The cattle dealer was at home in the district of Czernowitz where all good and decent people lived, and this young man with an un-Jewish, small moustache was at home nowhere and everywhere, but in particular in the coffee-houses of Vienna, Prague, and Budapest. The two families had nothing in common. Yet the marriage took place in July 1921, and when Mechel Leib saw "his daughter happy" (he didn't care to wait to see anything else) he went back to Snyatin to die.

At about the same time my mother's brothers Chaim and Solomon, just discharged from the Army and prisoner-of-war camp, left Vienna with waggonloads full of merchandise. They had bought up anything they could see ("I was a sea-merchant" is the joke). In Czernowitz one could sell every-thing. From coat hangers to irons, hot-water bottles and fry-ing pans, women's dresses and children's shoes. What Chaim, the eldest brother, did after they sold their last coat hanger I never discovered, but Solomon, the younger one, started to buy grains and chicken fodder and ended up in the import-ex-port of eggs. Solomon paid frequent visits to Vienna to see his sister with suitcases stashed with salamis and jars full of chicken fat. Later he sent his wife to have her leg amputated by a famous Viennese specialist because of an open tumour that smelled like a garbage heap. Aunt Pepi lay for long weeks in our living room and enticed us with sweets and pennies to kiss her (which we did with two fingers on our noses). My mother in true, self-sacrificing Birnbaum tradition made her bed and emptied her bedpans. The women chatted and sighed

27

together, and as my father was mostly away, I think my mother was glad to have company. The dying leg of the good old days in Snyatin and Czernowitz was their bond.

Rosa, what's new in the outside world?

Nothing.

And for three hours they went on talking about nothing. The word nothing held a special fascination for me. Back in the old house in the Ennsgasse, there had been a high fence across the road.

What's going on there, Mama?

Nothing, there is nothing over there.

How do you know, Mama?

There is nothing, I told you, and what does it matter anyway?

Could we never find out, Mama?

How can we find out?

Let's go to the roof and look down, Mama.

We can't go to the roof.

Don't we have the key to the attic?

There is no attic.

But there must be an attic?

Maybe there is an attic. But why should we go all the way up to the attic? What is it you want to know?

I want to know what's over there, Mama.

I told you — nothing.

Why don't they let us see it if it's really nothing?

What is there to be seen?

What does it look like?

Nothing, looks like nothing.

My dream was to climb up the stairs to the top of the house, twist my way through dusty cobwebbed junk, open the small window, and see for myself what this nothing looks like. And in my dream I went up the stairs one quiet, late summer afternoon, when people were asleep or at work, opened a door, and twisted my way through an undergrowth of dusty junk. That's where I saw first, what I believe is now in the mind. The little window hadn't been open for quite some time. I hold it above my head with a rusty iron bar, hands trembling. The houses and roofs had lost their colour, there was little to see, and absolutely nothing behind the fence. Just a hole and even of that one could not be too sure. Nothing. My mother was right. Nothing is nothing and where there is nothing

28

there must be something, the invisible must become obvious — sooner or later. My good and saintly mother taught me to trust my eyes and brain: nothing is nothing. She gave me knackwurst, rolls, mustard and salt-pickles she did not give my sisters. I was her only son. Her left breast was the Euphrates and her right the Danube. In her background was a small river called the Pruth, a west Ukrainian backwater, but her front overflowed with love for her children and love for the God of her father Mechel Leib. Like most Jewish women in love with their fathers, she thought her son had to be not only something better than her husband, but as a younger issue of their daddy, sons had to be at least brilliant and if possible genius. One way or another they were marked to become doctors. Mothers could not be disobeyed. I was obviously born "not to be a tramp, but to achieve something in life" — the least I could do for her was to want to be a doctor. A doctor of medicine, a respectable profession with a reasonable income. I didn't mind being a doctor just like our cousin Michael Gold from New York. He had come from the other end of the world to study medicine and didn't look crumpled up with arthritis behind a waistcoat with gold watch. He ran around in shorts, he wore pullovers. He liked to play football. He seemed human enough. I wouldn't have minded to feel a girl's pulse and put my head on her left breast. I wouldn't have minded at all to check on Erika Kindl, Sonja Auerbach, and Trude Wedeles. There was nothing wrong with the numbers 9-10 and 3-4 underneath your name at the door. I had different problems. First of all, I really wanted to be a clown in a circus, a serious man who makes others laugh, and besides, the reports at the end of each year in Primary School were so depressing, my mother was seriously convinced that Hartl had made a mistake, or, as she gradually admitted, might have a special grudge against his Jewish pupil. How could *her* son of whom even the teachers said that he was bright, who locked himself in his little room surrounded by books, be such a hopeless student? How this was possible I couldn't explain either. I tried to understand, but didn't understand, because there was basically nothing to be understood. For me there was no relation whatsoever between school and real life. I just didn't really want to go back to a hospital ever. Not as a patient and not as a doctor. A hospital was dull and dreary afternoons amid outcasts who cry in their pillows. Waiting for twenty-

29

three hours for the one hour between three and four in the afternoon, when they might or might not see their parents. When visiting hour approached, the nuns released us from the belts with which we were tied to the iron bedstead during the hours of rest and sometimes even at night for attempted masturbation. A sin that must have got INRI on the cross above the door. Like him we died every day with outstretched arms a very slow death, freed from this torture only because an angel arrives in time to take him down from the totem pole. It wasn't my mother's fault that I had to spend three weeks in hell, it was Freddie Grünblatt's fault: he had hit me by accident in the right kidney, I urinated more than a litre of blood, was rushed away in an ambulance, and was made to regret all the other games I had played with Freddie. He had sucked my penis and was about to force me to do the same to him. At the age of seven this was no longer considered a minor offence. I paid my sins in blood. "May His blood pour over you and your children." I learnt to understand what the Christian religion is all about, in a few weeks in hospital. It certainly was about suffering, blood, flowers, crosses, and little biscuits shared out by the hospital priest. I knew all about the Church and all about hospitals when I left, I had no desire to find out more about these two institutions. I don't want to be a doctor, Mother, I want to be a clown. It's too late now to say this, it was already too late in 1937. I had to be "something". I had to pass an exam to enter Gymnasium.

To enter the Gymnasium (a Grammar School) is to enter a living room of better furniture, a cupboard full of better food, and a coffeehouse full of smiling faces, which shout "Herr Doktor!" as soon as they set eyes on you. A Gymnasium is supposed to turn out better human beings after eight years of polishing your language and brainwashing your superstitions. It teaches the trick of all tricks: accumulation of facts and half facts, knowledge, for short. Academic knowledge "opens all doors" — you are a doctor after a few years of University — like it or not. It is idle to speculate whether the IQ of educated people is the hand on the weighing machine of money and honour, or a combination of both. Knowledge of Latin, Greek, mathematics, geometry, and history is supposed to be useful. It took me practically twenty years to get rid of this insane assumption. Twenty years to ponder my own value with regard to "really educated people", people

30

with eight years' Gymnasium and another eight years' University. The school of "life" was too common a classroom to regard it with any respect. After all, everyone has some sort of schooling until the age of fourteen. The police take care of that. No authority in the world forces you to be Herr Doktor. It's a privilege you have to struggle to obtain. My poor father, it was said, didn't have a chance to see a school from the inside after the age of eleven. The lucky man.

My mother found Berta, the daughter of her second cousin, to help me, herself, and Berta. I would not be a poor travelling businessman. I liked the idea. To be called a Gymnasiast was like Herr Professor — not quite the same but similar. Would Herr Professor like to join us tonight in our private box at the Opera? Would Herr Professor like to take his tea in his study? And how is Frau Professor? How is the mother of Herr Professor doing? Not many people were addressed in the third person singular. Only Doktors, Professors, Ministers, Cabinet Ministers, Dukes, and Councillors. Herr Geheimrat, a private counsellor, was the goal — but first of all I had to make this entrance exam to get through the door at the Chajesgymnasium, Staudingergasse. The Chajesgymnasium was a Hebrew Gymnasium. Hebrew was obligatory together with Latin and Greek and French and English. A child educated at the Chajesgymnasium? There was no better fortune to be won in this world. First I said: No I don't want to study with Berta. After a little pressure I gave in. How could I hurt my poor parents like that? Children are not allowed to hurt their parents. Twice or three times a week I crossed the Reichbrücke with books under my arm and pencils in my pocket, ready to be a "good boy", deep inside convinced that I would never pass the entrance exam anyway and afterwards everyone would leave me in peace to become a circus director or a vagabond.

How Berta managed to make me understand triangles and maths I don't know. Lemon tea with bread and chicken fat helped. I took it seriously, it seemed. I also had a good opportunity to walk around in the Prater after lessons. I passed the exam. Everyone was delirious with joy. The so far miserable fortune of the family took a distinct turn towards improvement in July 1937. We seriously discussed the kind of apartment I was going to furnish for my parents. I certainly would soon have made enough money to get my mother a help in the

31

house, buy her silken dresses and jewels, and purchase a Mercedes for my father to make his travelling life a bit more comfortable. My eldest sister Elli would get a place in town to do fashion designing, because she liked copying models from newspapers. My second sister Mira would have her studio and all the oil colours in the world because she was the best in her class at painting children, dogs, and Father Christmas. My youngest sister Ditta, who didn't know yet exactly what she wanted to be (at the age of eight!), would for the time being have to do with a new piece of chalk and a jumping rod. I was all set to save the family and ready to put up with a lot of nasty homework and inquisitive bullying by five or six different teachers. Not entirely without results. Professor Klein, who had the tip of her nose missing, taught us Latin, and I can still remember anytime anyone mentions the word Latin that "words ending on *-cis, -quis, -nis* are *masculini generis* as well as *mensis* and *orbis, colis, lapis,* and *pulvis.*" From Frau Professor Rosler, a lush lady in her mid-thirties, I know that Bolivia exports tin, China rice, and England steel. Thirty years ago, that is. From Herr Professor Gelernter, an excellent target for paper balls, drawing pins on his seat, and dirty words on the blackboard, I learnt that *shalom* means Hello in Hebrew; from Professor Keller, the director, I know that there is such a thing called hypotenuse, but what it is I can't tell. Professor Löwenherz, the kindest and most democratic of all professors, taught us the most difficult of all magic: to draw a person to look just like this person and not like some other person. Löwenherz sat down next to us on the bench. The other professors remained on their little stage in front of the blackboard from where they talked for about forty-five minutes without interruption. They talked me out of my daydreams. I probably knew in the first six weeks that I would never stand it here for eight years. The family would be disappointed. I was a total academic failure. A fraud among all the professors of the world. My position at school was in fact soon so hopeless, I dreaded every single day. I was a bad pupil. "Not really bad" as Professor Keller put it to my mother, "very intelligent even, I would say. But ... he doesn't listen and he doesn't work." The family was rightly depressed. I had promised so many good things and it didn't look as if I would ever be able to keep the promises. The only other subjects I was good in apart from German language, in which I was more or less the best in the class, were history and geography. History only required a vague memory of dates and names, and geography, like the collecting of foreign stamps, was a cheap way of travelling around the world.

My mother tried to be proud of my only achivement at school — the best in the class at essays and stories — but there was sadness in her voice, a skepticism of writers and poets. Without mathematics you can be a writer, that's true, but what kind of secure life is that? Little did she know that her skepticism on the secure position of a writer made me want to be "an artist" more than anything else. A poet, a writer, an artist was someone involved in this world only through the medium of his art. It was the only kind of profession where knowledge was not acquired from the outside, you had "talent" or you didn't. I never dared to tell her openly, in order not to "hurt" her, kept my secret to myself, and hoped silently that some sort of interevention of fate would save me from schooling. There were only three or four things good about school: to travel by streetcar with a special season ticket you could wave in front of the conductor, to write essays and stories, to draw with Löwenherz, and to preside over the members of my Radical Socialist Party, which I had founded in the class. After thirty years I still recall their names: Jankl Brenner, Haptschi Helfgott, Hanni Adler, Pepi Schmetterling, Gerti Deak. I had the prettiest girls in my club, something to get up for at seven every morning. Drawing with Löwenherz had also Löwenherz philosophical side to it. He wanted us to draw the anatomy of a person, just like the illustrations in the medical encyclopaedia at home. From the pages of this encyclopaedia I lectured to the girls of my club (and others if they wanted to listen) on the "facts of life". The "facts of life" were the male and female sex organs, the cycle of menstruation, the birth of a child. Löwenherz wanted the anatomical man straight, no sex organs. Is it conceivable that man inside is really full of red lines and blue and pink bubbles? The death-skull and the skeleton as we saw them in the Prater on the ghost train, are they really the core of man? A nasty awareness, in time you accept it. Water and bones and a bit of skin, a hole to eat and a hole to piss and a hole to empty his bowels. Löwenherz' anatomical lessons made me wonder whether Zionism is the answer for Jews and Socialism the last word on the betterment of the human condition.

Afraid to be called squeamish and sentimental, I would never have told anyone that my convictions, my ideals were being destroyed with red (for veins) and blue (for inner organs). Even the skeleton of a chicken made me "think". I buried chicken bones in the ground. The ants turned it into parts of a skeleton. *"Actually* we all are skeletons as you can easily see for yourself," someone lectured me. We are not Zionists and Jews — but skeletons. Not Austrians and Nazis — no, skeletons. Everyone is a skeleton, born with a small skeleton and dying with a bigger one. The skeleton is the root of man. You find them both in the ground, not imaginable until exposed, not visible until dug up. Richard Löwenherz (a namesake of Richard the Lionhearted, a prominent non-Jewish Palestine explorer), teacher in drawing, taught me philosophy, taught me to think about man, as if by mere thinking we could change him. I didn't learn Latin or Greek, nor geography nor mathematics; the Gymnasium taught me only one thing, not listed among the subjects of grade one: "thinking about man" or "serious thinking", as we used to call it. Between ten and eleven I started on this new investigation. Literature and who is who and who wrote what was no longer a topic for conversation. By the time I entered Gymnasium everyone had either read or heard about Dostoyevsky and Tolstoy and all the other great men. Between ten and eleven it was time to start thinking. What is man *actually?* was the prize question to which there were as many answers as boys on a bench in the Augarten. Every speaker started invariably with the phrase "In my opinion ..." or if he wanted to be a bit different, he would start with "If you ask me ..." The question of who man "actually" is, led straight to the question of what God "actually" is. We no longer discussed the fact that Jesus "actually" is a Jew and the Goyim should actually be glad that we the Jews crucified and by this sacrificed him or they would have remained pagans. We did it for *them.* This was beyond dispute. We no longer discussed a particular Jewish God or a God who looks like your grandfather. We discussed the idea of God. Why does man need God? Why does man create God? God obviously had not created us or he would let us live forever. Questions for atheists only. The religious boys, the cowards, never entered the debate. They dared not, unless there were enough of them around. With one or two of them one could cope, four or five were too many; they supported

34

each other like a football team, while we the atheists not only fought their religious fairy tales, we also fought one another. Not to believe needed strength of character, required the quick presence of mind not to get caught saying "God beware" or "My God" or "God help me". There was always someone around, friend or enemy, to remind you that a self-professed atheist had no "right" to talk like that. From my mother I had only very scanty information on the subject. "If you believe it," she said, "there is a God, and there is a God because you learn to believe in Him."

How do you know, Mama?

One doesn't *know* God, one *feels* God. You must feel God!

God knows how hard I tried. I went for lonely walks, sat an hour or so quietly in my room; I even prayed silently, "Please God, let me feel you. I want to feel you, God." I felt absolutely nothing that I wouldn't have felt anyway at that particular moment. Hunger or thirst, a desire for sweets and for girls. If anything, the thought of the "high and holy" usually turned my mind to girls and dirty limericks. (And I still like to make love with Bach and Buxtehude in the background.) The God I wanted to "feel" was the mysterious power over life and death. To prove his nonexistence we ridiculed the biblical tales as "scientifically explicable"; God was clearly psychological phenomenon. We didn't call it that. We called it "your fantasy" and this we could not "feel". It was easy to see the "advantages" that went with religion. Watches and new suits for bar mitzvah, a ride in an open fiacre for Catholic children on their day of confirmation. If anything, religion looked like a magic rite, a fantasy that somehow produced new football boots and bicycles. The atheist was the ascetic, the real saint, part rebel and part hero; his only reward: righteousness. I knew I was right not to believe in an invisible God. The invisible cannot be prayed to — there is no need to worship your own brain, that's idolatry. Religion is idolatry, I figured out. "God is an old man, don't shout too loud at him" was my father's verdict on the issue. But if God cannot exist and man is "actually" a skeleton, what kind of world is it we live in? It looks like a world without substance, a world without essence, and maybe a world even without human existence.

At nine or ten I had wanted to be Prince Mishkin, Dosteyevsky's idiot, I had wanted to have his mildness, tenderness,

35

forgivingness, kindness, that's why I probably always felt the opposite. I concluded that you can't be what you want to be at the same time. Those who want to be a Mishkin cannot be a Mishkin, on the other hand you could become anyone if you cease to want to be what you are not. But why Mishkin, and not Raskolnikof? Because Mishkin was strong and cool while Raskolnikof was cunning and confused. Because Mishkin was full of love and understanding while Raskolnikof was full of schemes that would lead to murder of an old woman. And while Mishkin was saved, Raskolnikof was condemned and damned for all time. At Mishkin they might laugh, but they would love him. Raskolnikof would be judged and punished.

I wanted to be a Christlike figure, a Christian, a good for-giving soul, a Christian among Christians. Prince Mishkin, the patient, peaceful, gentle, humane idiot, in the world of greedy, cynical, wealthy, nauseating bourgeoisie, was the lone hero. I too was totally on my own. I never thought there were people who cared for what's important to me. Nor did I par-take in anything of importance to them. I was not the outsi-der. On the contrary, I believed it's they who were the outsiders, and the centre of the universe myself in every single disguise. I could not follow. I could either lead or do nothing at all. I was either going to be in the front line, or not going to come along. I was put down, put back, put in a corner; not because people didn't like me, in fact they did — I was considered highly amusing and witty company — no, they just ordered me to fall back in line when I tried to take over. I was too far ahead, or too far behind. No one would ever be alllowed to walk beside me. I would be a leader, someone special; a figure to most, a friend to very few.

Is it that I couldn't stand others? Is it that I hated or des-pised them? Not really. I knew very few people I hated or des-pised. On the contrary, I loved people in company; without them I could not lead. My private self-assurance to be a leader was based on no visible evidence. No special courage, dis-tinguished background, extraordinary financial funds, exqui-site looks, no extraordinary warmth or saintly attitudes. Having no virtues to claim and not even any particular vices to be damned for, I made no claims at all, I just assumed. I assumed to have been thrown out inte the wilderness like a lone parachutist waiting for the rest of the company to follow suit. I myself would never set out to find the company.

36

The company had to find me. A lonely position. An isolation even in a world I could rightly call my home. I was critical of practically everything; nothing ever seemed right to me. Was it? But could it possibly be right if it wasn't right to me? But who is this me? To the outer world I did not seem frightened; I don't remember ever having been afraid of ghosts. But there was a time when I insisted on leaving all lights on, in the hall and in the bedroom. And that the lights in the toilet should stay on all night because I might not find the switch. Yet at other times I felt quite well in the dark, played games in the dark, sat in a dark room waiting for my sisters to enter the dark, hiding in the dark and not being seen — they had to shout "Where are you?" while I could see with one glance where they were.

Darkness I loved. I was not afraid of it, providing I was alone in it, providing it had been my decision and my own curiosity that made me want to be alone in the dark. Alone I felt strong; the company of people frightened me. I was not frightened of "nothing". I still believe that the mother is the spirit of the man — or the other way around.

In myself, in my home, in my immediate surroundings there is a long, dull, dreary summer afternooon that frightened me, maybe because others went on holidays and we never did. Once I did go; I was nine years old, in the summer of '36.

The place was called Kobersdorf, in Burgenland, the most eastern county of Austria — a children's holiday camp organized by the Zionist Youth Movement, Barak. We slept in a barn, washed in a spring, and had campfires in the evenings. I had some difficulties with the other children because I used to grind my teeth, and others couldn't sleep and complained. I wasn't unpopular, yet they made remarks like "You can't sleep next to him." I tried to make up for it by telling amusing stories, by imitating accents; as an entertainer I was immediately outside the company, felt "I'm different." Couldn't say exactly how, why, or where, but different, different views on almost every single topic. In politics, one of the big issues of our lives, I was partly for Socialism providing it was as radical as anarchism, as well as for a well-organized conservative state. A schizoid view maybe; now I am not so sure. It is not as insane as it sounds. I was for state control of the economy, for the equal distribution of goods, like bicycles, footballs and chewing gum, at the same time for a rigid class

37

distinction between people who will enjoy all those benefits of a Socialist society and the intellectuals. Intellectuals are people with minds,fantasies,and abstract notions of right and wrong. They would not benefit so much from material advantages, but receive in exchange the honour and respect of the people. They would not be allowed to intermingle or intermarry with them, but remain separate. They would be a totally self-contained world on their own, unapproachable like cabinet ministers, and write the laws. Their very words would be law. It was not a tyrannical society, it was not a dictatorship, was not run by a single ruler who could wash his hands in the blood of those people. It was my dream of a just society we, the Jews, needed more than anyone else.

When the Germans marched into Austria one Friday morning (Friday the thirteenth!) God lost his last chance to be recognized by me. The war against the Jews began practically the next morning. By Saturday all of Vienna was one big swastika. If *that's* what God wanted and everything is supposed to happen with God's will,God must be some kind of evil monster. Half Krampus the Devil and half fire-spewing dragon, and yet the same God (the Germans, the Devil) did also some good. He gave me the excuse I had been waiting for not to show up at school too regularly. Homework, thank God, had definitely become a waste of time. The town had more to offer than Latin in phrases and hypothetical triangles. Nazi slogans shouted in chorus and battalions of marching SS and SA men were a beautiful and exciting lesson in philosophy, politics, and sociology. A Czech called Navratil was an Austrian, a Croat called Globcenik was an Austrian, a Pole whose name one could hardly pronounce was an Austrian. Italians, Hungarians, Rumanians — all of them Austrians. But not a Jew with a good German name like Landwirth — no. A Jew was not an Austrian. A Jew was a vulture, pig, pig-dog, dog, subhuman creature, criminal, liar, monster; after March 13 he was all that and worse, officially. A new awareness started.

Why should they love us? was one of my father's favourite arguments, and the other was: What kind of world would it be if a Goy would feel inhibited to call a Jew a Jew? Didn't we call Goyim *Goyim?* Hungarians — *Nemtudoms?* Rumanians — thieves? Italians — *Katzelmacher* (which is something like an unreliable, doublefaced arse-licker)? He accepted it, to be a bit different, a little more discriminated against and didn't mind. My father said, "Vienna is Vienna and Jews are Jews. Black is black and Jew is Jew because we could not afford to be anything else." But what are Jews? Mother didn't eat lard or bacon, she must have been Jewish all right, but my father liked both and so did we, all four of us. Not rabbit, not pork, and not shellfish. But ham and bacon tasted fine. We couldn't have been real Jews. My father did not look Jewish, my mother did not look Jewish, we did not have Jewish noses and we had good German names. How the hell did the other kids know that there was something wrong with us? What was wrong with us was that all Jews are aristocrats, even swindlers and *Luftmenschen*. We had "given" the world Christ, Marx and Freud. We have the oldest culture in the Western world. We are exclusive. To be different and to be hated means to be chosen. Chosen to suffer and chosen to do great deeds. Austria is only a waiting room. For Zionists the point of departure. The final stop is Jerusalem. *Juden raus?* The Zionists had been shouting just that since Theodor Herzl suggested we should have our own state, just like the Serbs, the Czechs, and the Magyars. We belong to Palestine, wherever that is. If Hungarians, Poles, Slovenians and Czechs, Slovaks and Serbs need their own state, to run their own affairs, so do the Jews. Long before there were Nazis there had been a Zionist movement. A Jew had a choice to be either victim or "master of his destiny." He either was constantly being humiliated or he had to learn self-respect, that's the way the grown-ups put it. Viktor Rosenfeld, my instructor in religion, made me choose "self-respect" at the age of eight. He talked me into acting Matthatias, the father of Judas Maccabaeus, in a Chanukka play. I took the part because of the white beard that went with it, and ended up a member of the Zionist Youth Organisation of the "Jewish State Party" (*Judenstaatspartei*) called Barak (meaning "lightning"). When it turned out that the Jewish State Party was not a Socialist Party, but a party of the liberals, it was too late. I already wore their blue uniform. To all appearances I had sold my Socialist principles for a uniform. A blue shirt, blue pants, and blue soldier cap with a silver menorah cockade. I earned the small strip on my lapel for knowing the dates of all past Zionist congresses by heart. I had a leather shoulder strap, a leather belt, and a silvery cord for a whistle. We learned to march and blow trumpets, we could salute, sing and speak in chorus, and knew all the songs by heart. Learnt them just as quick as others. I would really have liked to be a soldier, but only a Jewish soldier.

My second hero became Josef Trumpeldor, a Russian of a very different kind. The tender Mishkin was an aristocrat and a Gentile; Trumpeldor a soldier, a Jew, a political figure, who had become a popular hero when he was killed at some lone outpost in the far north of Galilee. He was shot in the stomach, his guts fell out, he put them back with his own hands and sang: "Follow in My Footsteps," one of my favourite songs.

> At every hour of night and day
> you should remember me
> I fought and died for my homeland.
> All night long I ploughed the fields
> at night I shouldered my gun
> until the last moment.

In December '38 a train left for the Hook of Holland. There would be delays, unnecessary stops, certain difficulties, but "If I forget thee Jerusalem may my right hand wither." Embroidered on a silken white and blue flag around the golden Star of David, these words I repeated every night instead of the evening prayer my mother had taught me. A withered right hand would be even more shameful than patches on my trousers. The Jews vanished, most of them emigrated, but Vienna died when it destroyed its spirit in an act of autocannibalism. Jews and *Verjudete* had kept the doors of our German-Austrian culture open to other languages, minds, and tastes. The masses hated those who disturbed them in their lethargy. The National Socialist revolution was the revolution against the spirit of cosmopolitan tastes. Vienna can do without its "Jews". Look at it now. Behind a façade of comforts and pleasantries, behind a shopping window full of luxuries, behind the veil of elegant, sophisticated tastes, there is nothing but a yawn of eternal boredom. Vienna is a dead town, full of fat skeletons.

The Birnbaums and the L's, on the other hand, are a strong breed, or they could not have survived. If Jews seem

40

more vital and energetic than others, it's not surprising — no
other people went so often through the Christian mills of
"natural selection." The strong live and the weak die and
that's why all the Bernsteins and Fishbeins, Melzers and Hol-
länders are strong people. They are now in Melbourne and
Venezuela, Tel Aviv and New York, London and Paris, making a good or less good living. Business goes on as always.
We probably lost only eighty-four uncles, aunts, and cousins
in the last war. That's all.

School for Politics

Nine months I spent in schools and castles in and around The Hague, then they started to share us out to kind people. On November 2, 1939, two months after the outbreak of war, I arrived in the dickey seat of an old Austin, steered by another kind lady of the Jewish Refugee Committee, at a house with a garden in a quiet lane of a small town near Amsterdam. A Mrs. Van Raalte handed me to a Mrs. Van Son with a smile. It was late in the morning. Coffee time. The maid cleaning the house. Mrs. Van S. had five children of her own. The eldest was twenty-five and no longer at home, the youngest eight. There was a girl of my age ("You can play with her," etc.; when I did, a few months later, there was a scandal) and a daughter of twenty-one. With the son of eighteen, Jaap, I was to share an attic room. My new home had cupboards full of food, a piano, and a desk, eight rooms and a bathroom with hot and cold running water. What looked like tons of winter apples were stored under the roof next to our room. I liked my new home. It had central heating. There was no Mr. Van Son. He had died two years previously while playing the 'cello. He had beeen a translator, "an artist," the black sheep in a family of wealthy ink manufacturers. Mrs. Van S. was not good at anything, but all the same eager to play a share in the community of kind people. They had no money, which meant something different than at home. It meant her father, a tobacco importer, had to help, and they had to live on their stocks and shares. As a young Socialist I hated the bourgeoisie, as an individualist I didn't like sharing a room, as a Zionist I hoped this stay would be of short duration, as a foreigner I understood the language but not the humour; all I liked was to come back from school to a warm room and plates of food. The family was musical. Everyone played an instrument. The shelves were full of books in many languages. For the first time in my life I heard Bach. For Sinterklaas (the

Dutch Christmas) I received new clothes. I said continuously, "Thank you".

It was a very long winter with visits to relatives and cinemas. A kind of prolonged sleep before the real war would start. In this winter I read *Steppenwolf* and *Demian* of Herman Hesse. A vaguely mystical message from countries that couldn't have been on any map. I myself was living in such a country. I had no one to talk to, no one to confide in. What did we talk about? About the brands of different chocolate, about cigarettes, about a film one had seen. Banal, stupid conversations for me. Not serious. In Vienna we used to talk about God, the world, and the ultimate destiny of man at the slightest opportunity. Is man born with or without a purpose? interested me, and not whether he owns a Chevrolet or Austin, Is man's existence an accident like my presence in Parklaan No. 10 Bussum, or is there a deeper meaning to it? As there was no one to answer my questions, I started an imaginary correspondence with an imaginary friend. I wrote to him: If everything has its deeper meaning, deeper meaning must have deeper meaning too. Right?

His answer by return: Yet but no. Deeper meaning has only what needs deeper meaning. Deeper meaning itself doesn't need it, therefore the answer is: Wrong.

I enjoyed this kind of game like I had enjoyed football. The friends I had been running with after the ball would have been the same friends who would have discussed my philosophic questions at any time of day and night. I went on writing: If it doesn't need deeper meaning, why would the mind think of it? It surely needs something it produces and produces only what it needs.

He replied: Congratulations. You have discovered it.

The puzzle of deeper meaning was never solved, and I still don't know what it means. A loud and confused winter of '39-'40 followed. People were collecting money for the heroic Finns who fought the Russian invaders on skis. But all on the Western front was quiet. There were pictures in the papers of French and German soldiers exchanging Christmas gifts across the trenches. The Germans? Maybe Hitler (besides hating the Jews) wasn't so evil after all? Even Molotov seemed to stretch out his arm and say "Heil Hitler." And if the Communists, the arch-enemies of the Nazis, shake hands with them, Hitler must have made some concessions. Jews were still allowed to leave Germany and Austria by train and plane; even my parents had left by riverboat for Bratislava en route for Palestine. All I needed was a *certificate*, a British entry visa for Palestine; one for me and two for my sisters and we would soon be reunited.

Hitler is human, too, people said. Rattling our collecting boxes from one Jewish household to another, selling trees in forests with Hebrew names to anyone who wanted to help build "the homeland," the Zionist refugees worked a bit harder than the Dutch Zionists. Home was not only a country where Trumpeldor died and the *Chaluz* Pioneers danced a never-ending *horra*—homeland was where my parents are or would be soon. In this winter everything was possible. Anything could happen. A sudden telegram with a certificate. A money order from God knows whom, for the ticket. A letter in the familiar handwriting, starting with the familiar phrases, "My dear, my very dear children! Thank God," etc. As any one or a combination of all these marvellous things could take place at any moment, I was quite happy at school, got used to the outbursts of the eldest daughter in the house, who had taken an immediate and distinct dislike to me. I was ready to forgive Mrs. Van S. for being cold and haughty, hypocritically polite, and ready to forget that the world owes something to a refugee child (what I never quite figured out). There was a world war on, yet there was no war, only in Finland and Finland is far away.

The real, good anti-Nazi went on hating the Germans as if Ribbentrop and Molotov had never signed this friendship pact (a devil's pact, they called it). The Dutch hated the *moffen*, Nazi and non-Nazi, and that's why I loved Holland. Every Dutchman sided with the Jews. This was a good and friendly and a rich country. There was always money for ice creams and for cinemas, and one was free to say whatever one liked. Louis Polak, my sister's "father", a left-wing liberal, seemingly wealthy Zionist, took us both to see *The Wizard of Oz*, with Judy Garland. A peaceful, near-perfect world thrown into wild confusion by a technological monster that threatens and bluffs, frightens and horrifies and ultimately capitulates to innocence and shrewdness. Even Himmler is human, people said. The peaceful, quiet home-and-garden world might be the ultimate answer to all the problems in this universe. Universe. The word itself made me glow inside. A metaphysical hot toddy. What is the universe? Who made it? How did it come about? And again I wrote to my correspondent: URGENT. Please inform me by return about the structure of the universe. P.S. If there is a God let me know.

This was the answer: The universe is a primitive structure made of small particles called molecules and atoms. The highest form of existence is nonexistence or future-existence. It comes down to the same thing. Human enterprise turns this globe slowly to a desert of stone. Without human interference we would have reached this state before. That's all. Human existence is wasteful matter as far as the universe is concerned. Toil — called progessive — I call totally useless. All men should stop eating, working, procreating, and singing instantly and voluntarily. But if we cannot stop, then let's get on with it, three thousand times faster until the surface of this globe is covered by concrete. Colonies of computers (I am inspired by Franz Werfel's *The Star of the Unborn*) will soon take over. There will be war and calamities. The surface of this earth will soon be uninhabitable (Werfel, this Catholic Jewish Viennese is a prophet). P.S. to your P.S. God? God is my dachshund Laura or anything you fancy to call it.

Not wanting to take this message too seriously, I cabled back immediately: For Christ's sake, explain yourself.

And this is what I got back: Everything has a beginning, a middle, and an end. Though we don't always recognize which phase we are in. We presume there was first some organic slime (see your physics book). I think the slime was second. We are already the end. This life, not death, is the end. The beginning of all things might have been a human (a real human) brain the size of this globe that gradually dried up and in dying secreted this slime that grew to ordinary mortals. We are the end phase. The mind is a fungus, something that cannot imagine itself in its totality. Escaping total observation, it's invisible. What we see of it are the spaces it filled in. What we see is the differentiation of all organic and inorganic matter. The mind hides behind and in everything for the sole purpose of not revealing itself. Spinoza (I have just read him) is an old Jew. He talks about the mind of God — Ruach Elohim that makes things move. The mind (and God, Spinoza thinks, I think, are the same) manifests itself in everything and everywhere. The unimaginable must exist outside ourselves. That's his pantheism. For Spinoza, God doesn't have a long white beard; what did his grandfather look like? Like an ant? Like a tree? The breeze on the lakes near Leiden? No wonder they chucked him out of the synagogue. But I love him. His logic is as polished as his lenses.

Wrapped up in this news, I found it hard to continue as usual, and I hardly noticed the invasion by the Germans on May 10, 1940, and yet I had a strange premonition. I might even have caused it by an act of pure magic.

He promised me two packs of Wings if I could succeed. Cigarettes were 25 cents a pack. My weekly pocket money was 10 cents. For two packets of cigarettes I was ready to try anything. I had tried before but discontinued as soon as I felt some pain. Two packs of Wings were worth a little bit of suffering which wasn't that unpleasant after all.

Jaap lay in the other bed and gave instructions: Think about Fockie (the maid) shaking out the carpets. Can you see her thighs, her arse? Look higher up and higher. How are you doing? (He was moving under the sheets like a dog just out of water.) Come on, come on!

I wasn't doing too well. The pain started again and his talk irritated me. I can't do it, sorry, I said. Another time perhaps.

OK, said my teacher, I give you one more chance. Think of all the things I have mentioned to you, and the other things we talked about a few days ago. (He had told me in detail how he had fucked a girl on the heath.)

OK, I said. I will try again. Maybe sooner than you think.

The bet still stands, said Jaap, but don't try to fool me. I won't believe you until I see evidence.

What evidence? I wouldn't let him touch me. What the hell did he mean by evidence?

You know what I mean. He looked back from the mirror putting, as usual, half a pound of brilliantine into his hair. What I mean is you have to prove it. Do it in a handkerchief and show it to me. Is that a deal?

It was as good a deal as I could make. The same wvening, I thought of the Wings cigarettes (he kept twenty packs or so locked away in the drawer of his desk) and the pubic hair of one of my youth leaders, Adda Polak, which I had spied while lying in front of her in the grass. The picture was fading. It had been nearly a year ago. But I was determined not to be made fun of and to win my cigarettes. I had heard all kinds of stories about it. Blindness, madness, losing one's teeth. But the people who had been telling them had never impressed me with intelligence or authority. So I will be blind, I thought, closing my eyes. Blind forever and I won't have to tell anyone what I see. And with my eyes closed, Adda's hair turned into my eldest sister's hair, which I had once seen when she stepped over me onto the far side of the big family bed. I remembered the marbles in Erika Kindl's slit, the softness of my little sister's thighs (I must have been eight and she six). I remembered in a flash the pictures of kneeling and lying, half-dressed people a man had shown me and my friend one day on the way home from school; I could smell the heavy rose perfume of the pictures.

I came closer, it seemed, all the time to reality, to what I had seen only the same morning — Fockie shaking out the carpets and her plump short legs and heavy white thighs. It was all obscene, disgusting, forbidden — two packets of Wings tomorrow and Fockie's, not my own, hand stroked me violently, hurting me, as it were, on purpose. Hadn't Philip, Jaap's eldest brother, as Jaap told me, seen a man masturbated by two women in New York? And Philip looked strong and healthy and was probably the man it had happened to. And again and again Fockie, legs widespread in front of me. I couldn't wait much longer. Exhausted but happy with the success, I fell asleep, the evidence of my manliness carefully folded underneath the pillow.

Next morning at the breakfast table, morning music was interrupted by the voice of the newsreader. "German troops have invaded Holland. Fighting in the eastern part of the country is heavy. Parachutists have landed. The Queen advises the people to keep calm and continue as usual."

Well, there it was. Neither madness, nor blindness. Not the loss of teeth but much worse. Behind the privacy of closed eyes there is a vision of paradise. Take two steps across and you are at the entrance of hell. Try to dissolve for a few moments into nonexistence and reality will roar at you with insane fury. Sexual pleasure is a prelude for agony. While I was still floating in a strange, new, wonderful experience, the war invaded my sex fantasies, jumped down on me with the news of parachutists. Caught unawares by forces from outer space, I screamed (even the raising of a voice was normally

48

not allowed at table). "Let's go! Let's go! Let's take a boat to England. Immediately!"

Mrs. Van Son, like all her neighbours and the rest of the country, preferred the advice of her Queen to mine. "We have no visas, no valid passports, no bank account, and no apartment in England; besides, nothing can be as bad as the papers say. Everything will be all right."

The refugees knew what the Dutch still had to learn: Every day will be a trial. Every day and every hour one will have to be afraid to be oneself.

Things started to happen. The Germans turned a sleepy, fat country into a place of thrills and marvellous adventure. They issued all sorts of orders; alas, they did not apply. Not to me. I was not eligible for Civil Defence duty so I didn't have to care whether they wanted Jews there or not. Remobilization of the Army to be shipped off to prisoner-of-war camps? They may call up the Navy and Air Force as well, it doesn't hurt me. Everyone for himself and God for all of us. From now on I had to look after myself. Wonderful. Only the Germans in the country made me feel uncomfortable.

They are not that bad, people said. They are just like any other occupation army. A nuisance. An enemy. It could have been worse.

Could have been worse, Mrs. Van Bloem?

Yes, Mr. Van Hoven. I say it could have been worse. They are OK. They don't like the war. Look at them. They are nice boys, these Germans, though of course I hate their Hitler. But they can't help it. Soldiers are soldiers.

Right you are, Mrs. Van Bloem. My sister's brother-in-law's cousin had a German officer in her house. He has left now, was sent somewhere else. But he was such a nice man you could hardly believe he was a German officer. They are not all devils. They are human, too, Mrs. Van Hoven.

It was this that worried me. I couldn't say: They worry me because they are human. No one would understand. They may be humans to other humans, but they were not going to be human for long towards the poison of nations, the criminal scum that ought to be annihilated, the snakes that must be stamped out.

Let him talk, Mrs. Cohen, let him talk. Incidentally, did you know Hitler himself has a Jewish grandmother?

49

Grandmother or great-grandmother?

I don't know, but a relative who should know tells me Hitler is not kosher himself. Nor is Heydrich, and look at Himmler! I wouldn't be surprised if his name was Himmelfarb. Henschel Himmelfarb becomes Heinrich Himmler. What else?

Don't joke, Mrs. Aerdewerk, don't joke. They will get us all.

Oi, Mrs. Cohen, you are such a pessimist. What can happen? Will they kill us?

I didn't say that, Mrs. Aerdewerk. I didn't say they will kill us. But a holiday it wouldn't be either.

Which war is a holiday, Mrs. Aerdewerk?

A war and no holiday? School goes on as if nothing had happened. Will they finally stop teaching us algebra? (Who needs algebra now?) After the invasion of Yugoslavia they did. But I was impatient, did not want to take a chance; they might decide to let all Jewish children go to school forever. If those stupid Jewish schoolchildren want to walk, bicycles they don't need. Jews on bicycles disgusted every right-thinking German and Dutch Nazi. I walked. Three lanes to the left and one ahead. It was a fine and open school, a Montessori type of school. No work required, just fun. But not only fun. French is a difficult language. The sea battles of De Ruyter and the wars of Willem the II II are not exciting and hardly relevant to what is going on now. De Geusen fought the Spanish and won — but the Jews got burnt on the stakes and lost. Jews don't fight. Jews try to hide, try to get away.

Only in Palestine do they put their guts back when Arab snipers shoot them out. Let's fight them. Let's fight the enemies of the Jews. With hand grenades and machine guns. Let them not think they can kill us whenever they like. "Strength and courage, *chaver!*" was the greeting of the Pioneers. Our kind of "Heil Hitler". Palestine. Land of the fathers. (Whose fathers, who knows?) The land of the Jews is our land. I am a *Chaluz*, a Pioneer, a Trumpeldor. I will fight to the bitter end. I had to leave Bussum and Fockie, my algebra and my three meals a day. Good-bye to peace. The war is on.

To Zion we carry the flag,
the flag from the camp of David,

50

on horseback and walking
we are coming back.
To the land of our fathers,
to our beloved land,
the land of our youth.

This was our song. I had no desire to return to Vienna, ever — I wanted to go back to my beloved land, back to childhood in a Jungian subconsciousness. I didn't know that admission to the "youth farm," a school for gardening in the small cheese-town of Gouda, was not necessarily an affidavit for Palestine. (They will exchange the Zionists for Palestine-Germans — maybe — Mr. Cohen.) But if not, I could always console myself by masturbating under the shower.

Equipped with riding boots, big black riding boots like the German SS wore, riding boots made of soft calf leather and bought by mistake (we had wanted short boots for work in the fields) by Louis Polak, equipped with jackets, pullovers, shirts, woollen socks, and three large red farmer's handkerchiefs, I reported for battle early in '41. Ties were not on the list; a Socialist would rather hang by his neck than be seen in a tie. In Bussum I had shared a room with one eithteen-year--old masturbator, who admitted openly to his vice. In Gouda we were twenty in the dormitory of a boat that had run aground among tomatoes and beans. We didn't move beyond the potato patch at the end of the farm; the only movement was a silent, unsocialist, self-indulgent and unzionist, collective jerking-off.

The religious ran the place. They couldn't force you to pray, but they forced you to be around. Jews don't like to face the Almighty unless there are at least ten of them at hand. And if the ten didn't like the others to continue having a nice game while they had to face God with leather strips called *tvillim*, and little black boxes (called something else), everyone else too had to get out of bed, tuck in sheets and shirts, and report to a roll call in the courtyard, where a blue and white flag was raised. What a joke. It was soon stopped. Roll call at seven, prayer at quarter-past, breakfast twenty minutes later, subsequently dispersed among tomatoes, cucumbers, mushrooms, and apples to learn planting and picking for "later" in the homeland.

51

On Saturdays lengthy prayers. The religious were at the helm, the others followed. My first taste of Israel. My Jews feel they owe God some pious words and ought to read and go on reading forever what happened to Joseph in the dungeon and to Jonah in the whale. They read holy sentences and words from a roll of parchment called the Torah. I myself believed in nothing holier than a word of honour or a promise among friends. Like my father before me, I loathed the Orthodox. I hated the prayers and disliked the ceremonies. God, said Spinoza, is in every tomato. We had rows of them in our four or five hothouses. Why bother with God at seven in the morning? And no jokes allowed. Why let the religious get away with it? Because the goddamned Orthodox can make everyone believe that only they are good, right, and decent because they are with God, while we traitors are godless pagans. These self-assured bastards. Between Germans and Orthodox Jews, between intolerance and narrow-minded racial stupidity there was little to choose. If you have nothing to say to God, let people masturbate, for God's sake.

In the Schüttaustrasse synagogue, the local for us Jews of the Goethehof, I had loved God with his benign smile of Mr. Stock for a short spell, had teased Him frequently by thinking of cunt, fuck, and cock while pretending to pray. As He had not stricken me dead, I loved Him as one loves a teacher with a lot of bark and no authority. Now God was half a dozen teen-agers who knew all the prayers by hearts and shook in front of the parchment scroll like epileptics; I hated the mental illness that made them shake, the words they uttered, and the laws they preached. Thou shalt not this, thou shalt not that! God, Who let Hitler come to Austria, to Holland, and wherever else he liked to go, had little power to enforce His laws. I haven't forgotten the names of His fans either. Herman Frenkel, Norbert Stern, Chaim Friedmann, Berry Asscher, etc. I know them all. I loathed them all.

The small Gouda group (we were never more than fifty — of both sexes) was a mixture of Orthodox, semi-Orthodox, and atheists, good families, not-so-good families, and various nationalities. Where everyone is a Jew, it is a question of Poles, Dutch, Germans, and Austrians. Since I was an Austrian, the Germans teased me because of the way I spoke German. For the Orthodox, I am a Jew and therefore a traitor to the cause. Reading Hesse and Thomas Mann instead of loving to pick beans from high stalks turned me into the hated "intellectual." Nor did my background help. Poor Viennese Jews of Polish origin are generally despised as *Galizianers*. I felt ill at ease and didn't know where to go next. There was no return to Bussum and no way ahead to Palestine. Far from the flesh-pots of Egypt and nowhere near to the promised land.

In the desert I hoped for a miracle and the miracle came. The Germans performed it. In April '41 we had to put on a yellow star, on jackets and pullovers. The word "Jew" was printed black on yellow in the middle of a sextant. A conscious pioneer did not resent this marking. The star of David had always been our Hammer and Sickle, our Swastika, our Dutch Lion. It was a star of enlightenment. It spelled proudly, "I am a Jew." The Germans loved to know what these people looked like who ought to be destroyed like vermin. The Germans wanted "to see" the cause of all their misfortune as Siegfried had faced the dragon. After the yellow star, the concentration into two or three main towns.

Nine months before they all had to leave the farm for Amsterdam, I left. I was free. At last. Free and at large in Hilversum with a family called De Haan, where I had to share a bed with two other boys. By this time the rich Jews didn't care for poor refugee children; the Refugee Committee paid the needy ones towards the upkeep of children they took in, and by saving on margarine and bread, one could make a small profit on us. The De Haans had two or three of us in the house; we were permanently hungry. After Hilversum and the first taste of freedom I ended up for another spell of glorious freedom in a quiet family with a girl of my age in the vicinity of Amsterdam's Tropical Museum. I was fifteen, no school to go to, no job. On the waiting list to be called up at any moment to Work in Germany.

Our identity showed a big black "J" on a card to be carried on us at all times, to hook those who refused to wear the yellow patch. Shops, streetcars, cinemas were made out of bounds for us. The animals in the zoo were deprived of the sight of Jewish families. The Jewish theratre opposite was transformed into dormitories. Whoever could not prove by a special stamp that his life was contributing to the German war effort was locked up in the theatre and sent on to Westerbork, the next station on the road to Nirvana. The Jodenraad "protected" anyone who could think up a good enough reason why he should be allowed to wait a little longer. Diamond workers, textile workers, agricultural labour, and a lot of close and not-so-close relatives of the Jodenraad had a "deferred until further notice" stamp. There was no better amulet. If you are arrested and can show this stamp, you are released, you can go home and wait "until further notice". A matter of time. Sooner or later they would all have to go, but one rather goes next week than today. Thanks to my past "agricultural" war effort, I was "protected" by black ink. "Until further notice," however, didn't exempt one from hunger. Rationing of all foodstuff meant two or three slices of bread a day, a quarter of a pound of meat a week. I was hungry for bread, for cigarettes (no ration under sixteen), and love. None of it was available, then one day something happened to me, something strange, horrible, and insufferable.

I began to hate the Jews. Not only the Orthodox, but all of them. I hated their names, their faces, their manner of speech, their humour, and their nervous diligence. They were a rotten lot and one should get rid of them. Not because the Germans say so, but they say so because they are right. The Orthodox are an intolerant and hypocritical scum, the assimilated a bigoted and greedy crowd of petits bourgeois, the wealthy lived light-years removed from me, the intellectuals I hated, probably being one myself, but having nothing in common with them. There were the Zionists, but after Gouda, Pioneering struck me as collective masturbation under ill-equipped attics. The German Jews I loathed as Germans, the Dutch who hated us I hated back, the foreigners, mostly of Polish and Hungarian origin, were a slimy pond of gefilte fish. Shrewd and crafty and of Polish and Hungarian arrogance.

The Viennese hardly existed. They were in cabaret and in the coffeehouse business. *Mittelmenschen* — neither small fools nor great *chochems*. I wouldn't miss any of them. Except my sister, her foster parents, my foster sister Esther (but not the rest of the family), Fritz Sofer, a friend who had been with me on the train from Vienna in '38, and Heinz Mühlrad, another friend. Maybe there were another two or three just people I would have loved to keep in town — the rest could go. I hated the Jews because I hated the sight of death. Each of them was marked to be destroyed. I did not wish to belong to this kind of people. With glee and a certain pleasure

54

I watched them stepping into lorries dragging their parcels behind them, taking their screaming children and crippled old parents with them, taking their sick and dying on stretchers out of their hospital beds, taking the orphans with them, who anyway had little to live for, and taking some of the rich and powerful with them, to prove that this program called annihilation of the Jews was not guided by Capitalist class-consciousness.

Two Austrians were in a train between Vienna and Linz, long after the war.

"Hitler," said the one, "did everything wrong."

"Right," said the other, "he gassed the poor and let the rich get away."

"Right," said the first one. "Hitler was no good. If he had done it the other way round it would have been more fair."

Long before they needed the papers to live on, so they wouldn't have to stand in a queue to die, they needed money. In '38 and up to the outbreak of the war and even until the middle of '40, the masses of Jews could have left Germany and the German-occupied countries if there had been money to pay for their passage and money to resettle them in new countries. Too many books have been written on this subject. One of the best is *While Six Million Died*, by Arthur D. Morse. No need to repeat what everyone knows. The (South African) blacks can be treated like cattle by their white countrymen if they can't afford the price for equal humanity. Racial persecution is a matter of finances: "If there is no money, there is no money." "What can you do?" "It's not our fault, etc." People talked like that. In fact they meant: "If there is no money, I should have made money before and saved it for just such an occasion." "It's not my fault" meant exactly the opposite: "It's all my fault." But I, third child of a better family, had none of these self-reproaches, none of these self-accusations. It is *really* not my fault that they are being deported. If I had the money, I would help them; but as I haven't, I am not guilty.

Let them go and die, but all of them. There is nothing to fight with and nothing to fight for. What is it all about, after all? Opening another shop and yet another? Buying houses and selling them and spending the money in the south of France? What the hell did the Jews really want? To live? Just live for the sake of living? How can one want to live if one is born to die? But I didn't like it when I heard that a group of Socialist youngsters had been picked up to be crushed to death in Mauthausen. And I didn't like it when someone told me that Josef Bahr, whom I had known in Gouda, had been picked up. Josef, whom I had disliked the moment I met him, had been one of my worst enemies in Gouda. Now they were putting him to death. Better he could not expect, not the way Hitler and his party hated him. The death sentence for teasing was too much. I didn't hate the individual. Like any good Nazi I hated the lot. Not the Jew. "The Jews are our misfortune," it said in big letters on every front page of the *Stürmer*. Our misfortune? They are certainly mine. To survive this calamity I have to hate them; if I do not wish to die as one of them, I have to learn to live with the sentiments of the rest of the world. The rest of the world either hates the Jews or is indifferent to them. Those who love the Jews suffer, usually of some not-worked-out inferiority complex. I couldn't afford indifference. I have to hate because I love life. I love to remain among those who breathe.

I too was on the waiting list, wating for "further notice," but whatever notice the Germans would send me, I was going to ignore it. I could not write back: "Dear Obersturmbann-führer Rauter! Please destroy them all but leave me and my friends out." And I certainly would not obey. As they carried away more of these future six million, the town became alive — like an overcrowded rat cage. Everyone talked excitedly, people thought up fabulous ideas and had no money and no way to carry them out, people cried more and laughed louder. Something happened in the community that had never happened before—they cared less and less for their background, less and less for their possessions and degrees, they bothered less about their political and religious opinions, they became *one* people. "One heart and one soul," and later one big heap of charred bodies. A kind of preatomic fusion took place. A concentration of individual cells into a mass of sameness. The German idea of a *Volk* had given Herzl the idea of a Jewish *Volk*. Hitler united the Germans and managed also to unite these eternally quarrelling Levantines.

The notice, when it came, seemed to read, "And now, my good Jews, now you have learnt to live together peacefully, try how it feels to die together. There is no safer solution to the Jewish problem." It needed the genius of an Eichmann to provide the transport at a time when all wheels had to turn for victory. *Räder rollen für den Sieg* (All wheels turn for victory), it said on every railway station in big letters. Everyone was in a hurry. Some to get to Poland, others to get forged papers and reliable hiding-out adresses. The Germans were in a hurry to solve the problem and free the waggon wheels for victory.

Most Dutchmen kept cool on the advice of their Queen and faced the occupier "calmly and with dignity." On the whole they were not in a hurry to be sent to Dachau for hiding Jews or shot in a public park for taking up arms against the invader. I loved the Dutch patriots who fought and hated the Jews who were arrested. I needed forged papers, an address and rationing cards, and money to pay for all these luxuries. I needed contracts with those who held the cards and the addresses. The money I might get from Uncle Louis Polak. An identity card without the "J" was worth from three hundred to five hundred guilders (A hundred to a hundred and fifty pounds sterling). Not much for those who have it, but a fantastic fortune to a boy of fifteen whose only possessions are a few pullovers, underwear, shirts, two large red farmer's handkerchiefs and a black pair of riding boots. Had I stripped in the flea-market of Waterloo-plein, no one would have given me more than a hundred guilders. At least two hundred more were needed to buy myself another chance.

Things moved fast. Stalingrad was the first defeat. The Russians were after them, the *moffen* were losing the war. Against the Jews and the Dutch they still had a fair chance to win it. The eight o'clock curfew kept resistance men and Jews off the streets; the rest of the population seemed not to care too much about this inconvenience. Food, fuel, and medicament were the problems. I remember the smell of pot in the streets. Anything that would burn was rolled into cigarette paper and lit up. With every new lowering of rations the price shot up. In 1942-1943 a packet of cigarettes was worth ten dollars. Maybe it was even more before Stalingrad when the Refugee Committee found me a home with Mr. Jaap Granaat at Niersstraat No. 1, in a modern part of Amsterdam South. Granaat, thirty-five, married, with a small baby and a mother in the house, was an accountant, temporarily unemployed. His non-Jewish bosses had had to discharge him and there were not enough jobs going around among the Jewish firms. He was a bit of a Zionist. He must have loathed my Socialist fantasies, but he was decent enough never to make fun of them. It was a clean, modern flat, comfortable, neither rich nor poor. Two small German boys were in the house; they were ten and twelve. The Committee paid for their stay. Granny peeled the potatoes. Mother cleaned the house (no money for a Jewish housecleaner and non-Jewish women are not allowed to clean up a Jewish mess). Mother wrapped the baby in diapers.

Mr. G. went to day classes in a newly founded school where anyone for a little money could learn a proper trade. A proper trade meant blacksmith, carpenter, bricklayer, auto mechanic. Accountant and shopkeeper had been an improper business, the Jews now discovered. "What can I do with my accountancy in Germany?" Mr. G. asked rightly, adding to this kind of insane rhetoric: "But as a blacksmith they will need me everywhere, even in Poland." After six weeks of hammering away at white-hot iron bars, he came home proudly with a seven-armed candelabrum to celebrate the rising of the old heroes Maccabaeus and Bar Kochba against the Romans. To forge a gun and ammunition would have been more worthwhile under the circumstances. But who can tell? Seven candles to light up a fading memory of self-reliance might well be all that could be done. Granaat was an accountant, not a soldier. He was a family man, not a guerrilla. He had responsibilities and wanted to take care of his dependants, "even in Poland." How could he know that responsibility and hard labour are no credentials, no longer considered virtues deserving the price of life? He couldn't know, he didn't know, and he didn't want to know. He did his best. We tried the candelabrum and, by God, the candles fitted. The man had talent. An adaptable citizen. They don't let him on a streetcar and they push him off his bicycle, but he can still walk this three-quarters of an hour to the school and back.

Bored, sitting at home all day, or hanging out with the same few friends and wanting to be near the place where my love worked, I too went to the same school and took up metalwork. We had to saw innumerable pieces of steel and iron, and polish them, first with a file and then with sandpaper. They looked pleasant on the bookshelves. Besides, opposite the school in the Ghetto there was a hostel for nurses, and always a fair chance of striking up a friendship that could end in a dark corridor or on the floor of some dormitory. My love didn't want it yet. I loved Cilly Levitus. I met her at the Granaats'. She took care of babies whose parents were waiting in the theatre (across the road) for the next train to the camp. Cilly had brown hair, blue eyes, a turned-up nose, well-formed breasts, and a big behind. She proved her love to me with tins of potato salad she brought back from the nurses' kitchen. She looked like my mother and she looked after me like a mother. She wouldn't let me undress her and only once allowed me a glimpse of her firm breasts. I couldn't get her into any bed or corridor, but I could hold her hand and hope that one day she might forget her pious upbringing. I had never tried it, she had never tried it.

After a few weeks she allowed me to fondle her brests, after "we knew each other better." Once in the grass after crossing the IJ Canal on a ferry and once at home. The rest was game and fantasy. I don't want to be sixteen again and in love with a German-Jewish nurse with a big arse. I would (again) love her madly, eat out of her hand, potato salad and everything she offers, and wish to bury myself in her lap for all eternity. The poems I wrote for her sounded like my mother's, for whom they were basically written. I loved her firm steps, her firm grip, her insanely optimistic smile, and even her endless rattling on about anything that came to her mind. She was my girl.

My friend was Fritz Sofer, who lived in the town house of the Werkdorp Pioneers. Sofer hoarded cigarettes from his rations (he didn't smoke) and wanted me to sell them on the commission basis of one cigarette for every packet. It wasn't hard to find buyers for cigarettes. But his had turned mouldy after a long wet winter in a cardboard suitcase. They tasted disgusting. No one wanted them. I managed to sell twenty packets of this rotten tobacco, acquiring two full packets for myself. They made me sick but calmed my nerves.

New notices all over the town. Report for deportation: Letters A-K on Tuesday, L-P on Wednesday, Q-Z on Thursday. No on wished to go. The rumours spread grim tales. The Germans had to think up something new. To get them all in the end was a question of concentrating them first. The non-Jews in the old Ghetto had to move out, the Jews moved in. As the old Ghetto wasn't big enough, the Germans turned the Jewish part of the Afrikaner quarter in the new East into a new Ghetto. A few notices went up here and there, a bit of barbed wire was all that was needed. The Ghetto was open, not sealed off like Polish ghettos, but there were now more policemen in the quarter and anyone could be stopped and asked what he was doing and where he was going. As if anyone knew. Niersstraat in the new South was too good a quarter to leave to the Jews. Even for their last few months. We got notice to move to the Afrikaner quarter. Granaat found himself an apartment — which was not too difficult. People were leaving all the time.

In the spring we moved to Retiefstraat 39, less two members of the family. The baby had been given to farmers to look after until the war was over, old Mother Granaat was asked to stop peeling potatoes and go down to a waiting car by two polite Dutch policemen who carried her little suitcase down after her. The old woman had no stamp. She had to start work right away. It solved some problems. There were less quarrels in the house, two people less to feed, and two less people to worry about. There is no safer place than Westerbork, but safer still is to be dead, people said.

Jews, Jews, why did God create you? started one of my poems, a sentimental lament for all that is mortal. Flowers, grass, leaves, and Jews. Roses rhymed with death for the first time. The kitsch had become reality. The Nazis' romanticism had transformed life into kitsch and the small insignificant man into a tragic hero. The milkman and the travelling salesman had a face for the first time. Some went to die tight-lipped, others stared with triumphant melancholic eyes into the streets of Amsterdam. They had expected to run around this town forever. And battle forever to make a living. All this was superfluous now. They had struggled for their lives in the last moment by refusing to go — but they had lost. They were now going to face their defeat, dignified. Some of their non-Jewish Dutch equivalents carried guns, raided ration offices and town halls, liberated prisoners, shot black-listed Nazi officers from behind their beer — and the small man became the new tragic hero. An American, Arthur Miller, sang his swan song when he mourned the *Death of a Salesman,* and because of this play I count Miller among the great playwrights of all times. He had seen it for the first time. The age of the ordinary man began in the Second World War. A stillborn creature of whom we are seeing the last right now.

The banality of purpose, the taste of blood and death, the smell of burned flesh — I loved it all. I was sixteen, I enjoyed my walk in the sun and hated the world in its graveyard. Death was just an idea. Those who stepped on the lorries and those who were executed in the park, those who died drinking their beer — I saw them alive. I have never seen a dead man nor have many of my generation. The killing took place far away. We were left with a feeling that it happens, whether we see it or not. *It happens is all one needs to know*. One nursing home was raided, then another. All nurses to work in Germany. One hospital and old-age home was raided after another. All patients and all doctors, all old people and all those who look after them to work in Germany. The diamond workers received their notice and the textile workers theirs a week later.

And by now even some of the big bosses of the Jodenraad disappeared and didn't come back from their office. The babies opposite the theatre were kept behind for a long time as ransom. "Parents collaborate and go quietly — or we will do something to your newborn!" The Germans hated fuss. Then one day in June or July they sent the babies after their parents. Many of the nurses managed to escape and hide. They could run faster. When all must die, why feel sorry for babies? The poor and innocent babies? Were their elder brothers and sisters, their parents and grandparents more guilty? I even hated the children and the babies. They stank.

Back at school in Bussum I had known a boy called Rob. He was vaguely a kind of friend. They were poor at home, he had no father, we were both outsiders in the class. Rob, thought not Jewish, had moved from Bussum to Amsterdam. We met occasionally. I asked him to get me an identity card and told him I had no money. Three weeks later he got me the card. How I don't know. But even a half-blind man could see the clumsy attempt to change the serial number. The card was useless. Free is always too cheap, my father used to say.

The raids, called *Razzias*, were our "happenings." Every day another. Street after street the Ghettos were cleaned out.

The old Ghetto was gone. Next turn would be the new Ghetto in the Afrikaner quarter. The exact date no one could forecast. Some said Monday and others Friday, some guessed Saturday and others Sunday. They were all wrong. The last big raid took place on Thursday the 20th of June, my father's birthday, and started at six in the morning. I did not want to stay home. I was too excited. I went to see a girl of twenty-three ("an old hag") who lived on the Afrikanerplein just around the corner. Her name was Ilse Aronade, and she was married to a man called Günther. Both were German, both ex-Pioneers from the Werkdorp. I had met her in the Werkdorp house near the Zoo. Fritz Sofer and the others had told me, "Ilse is an open city. Any man with a penis has a chance. She can take three a day." I rang her door at about ten in the morning hoping to be the first. Her husband was at the school where he taught elderly shopkeepers to dismantle a motorcar. It was a warm summer's day, blue skies, with white stripes of high-flying American fortresses. The day had finally come. They will have to drag me from Ilse's breasts and remove me from her womb because that's where I was going to hide, right in Ilse.

I figured they wouldn't reach our street until later in the afternoon. There were still plenty of Jews to collect on the way, and later "We shall see, we shall see," said the blind man. Ilse was neither small nor tall, had reddish hair, and wore thick glasses. Her lips were twisted, she had beautiful teeth, a laugh that made me shiver, and a smell that made my hand moist. What shall I say? How does one start? "Ilse may I sleep with you?" "Ilse I love you." "Ilse help me, my erection won't go down." So I said nothing, I had come for lunch. I ate my cheese and bread, swallowed silently three cups of coffee, and tried to smile. We had been eating silently for nearly fifteen minutes when from outside came the sound of pots and pans being dragged over cobblestones, the crying of a child, the barking of a dog, the shouting of a loudspeaker, march music, and the tenor of a high-flying bomber.

We sat and ate our lunch. We didn't know each other and didn't know what to say. All we wanted was to find out what it feels like to feel each other. She started it. I was too shy. While I was cutting another piece of cheese she put her left hand on mine. Didn't she want me to eat her cheese? If she wanted me to stop eating her cheese, why not say so? I could

have eaten a horse or two at the time, and there was plenty of
cheese in the house. "Have you ever seen a naked woman?" It
stopped me chewing. I couldn't say no or yes with a mouth full,
and wouldn't have told her the truth anyway. I just looked
at her, kept on looking at her, and followed her with my
eyes while she disappeared into a small room adjoining ours.
The situation had reached the end phase. Mine in particular.
A few minutes, maybe ten or fifteen, and I would have to face
the ultimate test. I was not going to die in a concentration
camp because I was never going to go there anyway. I had to
face it now, now that Ilse in a dressing gown reappeared from
the small room and sat down on the edge of a bed staring at
me all the time through her thick glasses, staring at me until
my saliva dried up. I sat there and didn't dare to go on eating
— she might have considered it bad manners in this situation.
I wanted to piss and didn't dare to get up. I wanted to say
"Another time ..." and couldn't because there might not be
another. I wanted to come right there and get it over with. I
would rather have sat in her chair and felt ashamed forever
after, than get up and move towards the bed. She pointed a
crooked finger at me as old tarts do with young men in the
movies, and because I was a hero, a Trumpeldor, a Tarzan or
Tom Mix, I had to face it. I had to go through with it. There
will be no need to hide under an attic at five, in half an hour
or so she will have killed me and thrown me out of the window or down the stairs, and if she won't, her husband, who
had to be back at any moment, would. Good-bye, I am coming. I went to her bed, she opened her gown, my fly, frigged
my prick (how much better was her hand!), put it in something even warmer, a few moments, and I died in the park, on
my stomach, with eyes closed, just like the man in the Resistance. I died again and again and once more. My back hurt,
my bones ached, my head grew through the window right up
into the sky. White strips of bandage around my forehead, a
hero executed, I rose from the ground, buttoned away this
goddammned prick that had given me nothing but anxieties,
and took my jacket.

A key turned in the door. "I put it on the latch, don't
worry." She shoved me, throwing my shoes after me, into a
small bedroom next to the entrance. Günther kissed his wife,
said "They will soon be here. Let's go." At the word "go" I
rushed out of the door and ran down the stairs sliding along

the walls until I turned round the corner. (Little did I know that Günther couldn't care less what his wife did when he wasn't at home. They were all Pioneers.) Out in the fresh air, in the sunshine, walking slowly around the block and back to my room I started to breathe a new exciting life. I had passed the test and survived. All that was left now was to beat the police to it as well.

I don't know how I spent the rest of the afternoon. I was in no hurry. When the Germans enter the street, it would be time to disappear under the attic, nothing could be done before. I went to visit an old friend from Gouda. A boy whose name I forget, we use to call him "Fart," because whenever he was near, it stank. His father was a high-ranking ex-Army officer. He relied on his medals. If they came he would show them his medals, they will salute and leave. People believed in all sorts of miracles at that time. I had nothing much to say to Fart, I just wanted to say hello and good-bye. There was a chance we would never meet, and there was an equally great chance that we might meet somewhere in Germany. I was sure I would never see any of my friends again, not because I was going to die — but because they were. Fart's family sat ready to await the Germans, like any family that waits for the bride of their son. They were impatient. The suitcases stood neatly packed in the hall (thirty kilos were allowed and not five kilos more). Chairs and armchairs were covered with sheets to protect the furniture from dust, as they might not be back for some time. They had washed up the kitchen and polished every pot. The empty milk bottles were neatly lined up on the doorstep. That's the way they wanted to go, if amulets and medals wouldn't help — decently, neatly. Like the clean and correct citizens they had always been.

Not like the Poles and Hungarians who left everything in a mess: "Moishe Katzenpischer, the *shochet,* has destroyed his entire furniture, imagine!" said Fart's mother. "What a people! They even let their children help them. What a bad example to set children! Polacken, of course."

Remembering that I, too, was a foreigner, she apologized. You are not a Pole? she said.

I am from Vienna, I said. I would burn the whole quarter down if I could before I leave.

Her face froze. She coldly and politely offered me some

lemonade. The old Army officer gave me a glance across the table that said: Thank God my son won't be long in your kind of company.

If you get to Westerbork before me, give my best regards to Manfred and Schoschanna, I said, having heard that our hostel parents from Gouda had been picked up.

Where the hell do you think you are going? laughed Fart.

I don't know, I said, but we don't have the same way.

In fact, Fart survived the war (though his parents did not), but I never saw him again.

I walked home slowly, looking in every window. The Dutch don't draw curtains. Wherever you looked, the families sat gathered round their covered tables, some drining tea and reading the papers, children playing chess or dominoes. It was like a Sabbath. Or a Sunday. There was no rush. Jews have a lot of patience. For the Messiah they have waited three thousand years or so; two or three hours of waiting means nothing to them. I was so filled with hatred for my people, the Jews, I had hardly any left when I returned to Granaat, who, nervously helped by his wife and the boys, shifted the furniture from one room to the other. He had already changed round the living room into the bedroom and was busy clearing the furniture from my room. Where had I been so long? I could have given them a hand, instead of hanging around, I could have done something useful. Little did he know that I had never spent such a useful day in all my life. What useful work? "I managed to sell some of the furniture," Granaat said, "and tomorrow morning someone will collect it, so the Germans won't get it all."

His wife kept repeating, "But Jaap, they will seal the flat as soon as we leave."

"Never mind, let's go on doing it, we have nothing to lose. They might forget to seal our apartment. Come on, give us a hand" I helped him move my furniture out of the room. "But why move it around, Mr. Granaat?"

"Because I don't want him to waste time looking for the furniture I sold him. I told him we put it all in the front room." Granaat had taken off his jacket. His wife wore an apron, the boys their best Sunday suits. I wore my riding boots, riding pants, a dark shirt, and a jacket with a yellow patch. The jacket I had worn in the street I locked away in the cupboard.

"You look like an SS man," the boys joked.

"Never mind," I said, pleased that my disguise impressed them. I also had the black and red triangle of the Dutch Nazi Party pinned behind my lapel. It wasn't time yet to put it up front. It might have disgusted them. By half-past five we were finished with shifting the furniture and sat down for our afternoon cup of tea.

Then suddenly the noise of lorries was so near that we thought them to be around the corner. We finished the tea. Everyone took his luggage. Jaap Granaat locked the door on the latch and we went upstairs. Before we had all disappeared through the manhole, we heard the shouting in Dutch and German at 37 and across the road at 24. We sat down quietly at the back of the attic underneath low beams. Two blankets were spread over the floor and Mrs. G. had thoughtfully arranged a few pillows (taking off the pillowcases first, so they wouldn't get dirty.) We sat down and listened.

On the other side of the attic I saw a man of about fifty with a beard, a woman who must have been his wife, and three girls between fourteen and twenty. I couldn't see the girls very well, they were practically in the dark. I only saw the face of the man. The light from the small attic window fell on his head, covered with a yarmulke. He looked like a butcher. As I kept staring at this family, never having seen them before in my life Jaap Granaat turned around and whispered, "They are from Rumania; they live downstairs." What if they would only pick up the Granaats and the boys and the parents of the girls, and I would be left with the three of them in the attic? I have three sisters, nothing could excite me more than to be left alone in the world with three girls. If parents wouldn't prevent them, by their very presence, brothers and sisters would make love all the time. I was ready again, and they wouldn't have to open my fly this time. Let the grown-ups just get out of the way.

"All Jews out of their homes!" a voice shouted in the house. They shouted it in Dutch. A loudspeaker voice in Dutch and German added, "Whoever does not come down now, with his luggage, will be put on transport to a special punishment camp. This is your last warning. Bring your keys for your apartments with you and hand them over on demand."

The voices repeated the same things three or four times, and a few minutes later we heard one or two men going upstairs rattling and hammering at doors. They obviously didn't pay attention to the manhole, which was out of sight because of the low-hanging ceiling of the second floor. One would have to go all the way up to see it. So what the hell if one or two Jewish families get away this time? They will have another *Razzia* if there are too many left, next week. That's why the police didn't come all the way upstairs, and because in the late afternoon everyone, after a full day's work and unpleasant work at that, is fed up and tired. The police who came to arrest them did not hate the Jews, nor did their immediate superiors (the few among them who did are exceptions). From postwar trials we know: They were just doing their job. This is exactly what it looked like. The Jewish problem had to be solved; it was solved by lawful, legal means, not by a massacre, not by drunken Cossacks. Eichmann said he never hated the Jews. Hitler probably did. But it was not a question of hatred, it was a matter of law enforcement. They didn't come to kill the Jews, this was just an unfortunate logical consequence of a laudable task — to clean up a mess, to straighten out what looked uneven, to put order into chaos. It was not done with Asian-Oriental emotionalism, it was carried out with Lutheran cold-bloodedness, with the Lutheran compulsion to remove anything "dirty". If the Jews are pigs (whether Fart's mother does the dishes before her execution or not), Jews remain pigs. The killing of animals and the extermination of insects (that's what they called us, as well) are not inhuman. The wilful destruction of people would not have been palatable to the masses of Germany and the occupied countries. Living for generations among people who wish to wipe them out, the Jews were ready to be wiped out. They too believed in this final solution.

A few minutes after the last shouting had died away, afraid of special punishment, all of them went, one by one. That's why I stayed behind. I wanted to have nothing to do with these people, this bunch of remote relatives. Too familiar the way they sat huddled together on their wooden benches on top of lorries, the children on the floor playing with their dolls and toys and holding on to their luggage. This noise, this crowd — I wouldn't have liked to share a compartment with

67

them from Amsterdam to Utrecht; I was certainly not going all the way with them to Poland. They are a dull and boring lot, my remote relatives, with whom one can't exchange a single intelligent sentence. Typical relatives.

After the relatives had finally cleared out, I thought it safer to climb out of the small window and up to the roof. I couldn't have done it before, they might have objected. Two hours I lay on my belly, looking down through the attic window as if I were a scientist observing rare organic cells. But there were none left but me and my messy life. It was nearly dark, about ten; a flashlight from the roof across the street turned in all directions. Obviously they didn't see me. Half an hour later the whole world was as normal as on any other evening.

I went back through the attic window, tiptoed downstairs. The apartment was locked and sealed. The contents of this apartment now belonged to the Reich, to Eichmann and Rauter personally maybe, and no one was allowed to touch them. Stupid Jaap Granaat had thought Eichmann and Rauter would not know how to take care of their new property. I didn't want anyone to know that someone had been around, nor was it wise to make too much noise; anyway, breaking a door open without a tool is not easy. I went back upstairs, climbed over the roofs, down the drainpipe to the kitchen balcony. A few strips of light came through blackout blinds. The kitchen door too was closed, but I had to get in to get my suitcase and Rob's I-card from under the linoleum in my room. Besides, I was starving and had to go to the toilet.

I broke the small window, it sounded like an explosion, a light flicked on and off. On the stove were the leftovers from yesterday's dinner. Green peas. Half a pot full. I couldn't get my boots off, they hurt like hell, and I didn't want to walk around in them either, not because of the few non-Jews in the back yard who still had their lights on, they couldn't possibly hear me, besides, most of them were OK. I ate all the peas, tried for a while to pull the boots off, and as this did not work, and it became more painful to try to pull them off than to leave them on, I thought all might as well stay as it is. If I take them off, my feet will no longer hurt, and if I lie down on the bed, I might go on sleeping until noon. Better to sleep restlessly and wake up at dawn (without an alarm clock) than to run risks. At six the night curfew expires; I could be at the tram stop at a quarter-past. In time for the first Line 3.

I woke up at five to six, checked my few belongings in the small suitcase. (A suitcase had to be exactly the right size as people were continuously searched for black-market goods.) I pinned my Nazi badge up front, put on my grey hat with the rim down, tied a black tie over my dark grey shirt, and looked (in the mirror) like a Nazi home from a spell of duty. I put on a fierce look, and left for Line 3. I walked with military step, looking straight ahead of me. There was no one around. Office workers and labourers on the streetcar moved away from me. More than the Germans the Dutch loathed their own Nazis. In this outfit I wasn't likely to be stopped. Rob's I-card I had left under the linoleum. Better no identity at all. I could make one up better on the spur of the moment, rather than produce one that was so obviously faked. At the Munt I changed to Line 24 down to the new South, to see what had happened to my sister and her foster parents. I was a good, sentimental Jewish brother. They had all spent the day in the storeroom of their apartment. They looked a bit pale, otherwise well. I didn't want to stay too long; I shouldn't have come in the first place, my entrance might have been observed. I wasn't welcome.

I took a streetcar to Hemonylaan 20 where the Pioneers had their office in town. To my surprise there were at least a dozen yellow patches in the streets — the office was open and working full steam. I wasn't the only one who had got out of the raid; there were hundreds of others. Those who could possibly claim a Zionist relative now also claimed help. The waiting room had fifty chairs and fewer than half a dozen people. The survivors were scattered all over the town. Just like after an earthquake, many still too shocked to move from wherever they had been when the disaster struck. Among half a dozen survivors, with a background of Gouda, I was accepted as one of them. They were going to provide me with papers if I could find the money. They would have done it without the money, but needed every penny for conspiracy and bribery. I had to wait my turn and discovered that Ilse was waiting as well. When the two of us were left alone, I planted my right knee between her thighs and she stroked my penis to say good-bye. She must have been waiting for someone; when

69

I came out of the office she was gone. She and her husband survived the war but I never saw her again.

I don't know where I hung out before I was due to call for my papers and address at Number 22 Niersstraat. From the street where I had lived a few months previously as an Austrian emigrant and Jew, born in Vienna 10th February 1927, I left in the body of one Jan Gerrit Overbeek, born in Aalten, province of Gelderland, on 7th January 1926. I was no longer an Aquarius, but now twice born. The paediatrician who helped me to this new existence is a half-Jew from Germany by the name of Gideon Drach. The money for the identity card came again from Louis Polak, the foster father of my sister who was also something of a father to me. His spirit of generosity did not die with him. I would like to meet Gideon Drach again. I don't know what I would say to him. Can one say "Thank you" for being alive and cursed forever to explain existence as the result of an assumed identity? I don't even know if I am back from the war. This war has never ended.

I wish I knew where I stayed, before I left for Jutphaas near Utrecht. Probably with the two spinsters, Tante Kok and Tante Miep — who had several Jewish children in the house, most of them belonging to the family of Leo Laub, a thin, scholarly type who had been with me in Gouda. We used to call him Trotsky. Trotsky himself was somewhere else. Under the attic were three of the sisters; Esther, the eldest, might have been fifteen or sixteen, then Cilly Levitus and her younger sister. I had helped Cilly to obtain an I-card (with money from Louis Polak) and had taken her to a photographer in the Kalverstraat. She introduced me to this address in the Tintorettostraat. The aunts, in spite of the fact that they must have known all about sex, spending so many spinster years together, didn't think I was old enough for it, or the girls weren't old enough for me. I could only stay two nights.

Overcrowded hiding places are a bad idea anyway. I spent most of the time studying my face in the mirror. I had the card and a ration card and an address. I was Jan Overbeek, yes. But I didn't look like him. Not yet. My nose is straight, as straight as Hitler's, but there was something wrong with my eyes. Not the sight, but the expression. The Germans thought the Jew is attached to his nose — the Jew was in the eyes. The kind of Jew I could recognize without a yellow patch. The

Jew was a certain soft, reflective look. A look of shame and humiliation, a wise look, a pensive one. All this I had to lose as soon as possible and before I could take my suitcase to the Amstelstation for the train to Utrecht. I couldn't change the face, and there was no need either for me to change the face. The face is the eyes. I had to change my look.

It would have been easier if I had gone on hating the Jews as I had hated them only a few days ago, but now that my name was Overbeek and I was Dutch, I was also less of an anti-Semite. My new identity didn't cast me to be a Nazi; this charade I had only played for the first walk out from Retiefstraat. I knew I had to be an ordinary Dutch boy, with no hatred and no special emotions one way or the other. A young Dutch labourer by profession (as the I-card said) likes girls and cigarettes, movies and music. I had to be gay and indifferent, relaxed and cool. In short, one of them and not one of us. I tried to fix my look and finally ended up with a face that looked partly *hautain* into the world and partly nauseated. An ordinary Dutch labourer I did not manage to look, however hard I tried. At least not in my own eyes. I saw a non-Jew in myself, but a slightly peculiar one, a little soft on the edges, like a Dutch student and intellectual (which didn't fit Jan Overbeek who is and must remain a labourer). The kind of student a smart German or Dutch Nazi might suspect of being with the Resistance. Some of the things I saw in myself I probably wanted to see, like the intelligent non-Jewish student; other things I saw (the haughtiness and the nausea) because that's exactly the way I felt. I spent at least two hours in front of the mirror, until everyone complained about my using the bathroom for too long. I pulled my face into a hundred different faces and left the bathroom as I entered it, with hatred in my eyes. Hatred for the Germans. The Jews, now most of them had left, were of no importance to me.

I hated the Germans like a good Dui patriot would. The expression remained the same, as it wasn't too difficult to feel hatred for the *moffen*. I had always and spontaneously done that anyway. Not only had I hated the Nazis, I had hated the Germans, Jews, and non-Jews since the first day in the refugee camp when German children made fun of us children from Vienna. What I always disliked most about the Germans was, of course, their language. The way they used *our* language. Austrian as spoken from Prague to Trieste, from Bucharest to Salzburg, as it was spoken by people from Cracow and Budapest, Zagreb and Czernowitz, was the real German. Not only the ways the Jews spoke it — they mixed it with a lot of Yiddish phrases and words — but even the way any Austrian Nazi spoke German was a language I could understand. (That's why I still cannot read Günther Grass and Uwe Johnson, nor any of the other Germans, while at least I can understand the language of Peter Weiss who is Jewish and Enzenberger who spent most of his postwar years in Norway.) Part of the new face was to show hatred for the Germans or simply hatred. Overbeek was a not-so-relaxed Dutch labourer, but one who could stare any policeman dead and make any Dutchman move away from him, because to him Overbeek looked like a Nazi.

On a Monday morning among the throng of workers and office workers, soldiers and Dutch Blackshirts (the equivalent of the Brownshirts in Germany), I took a tram to the Amstelstation. It was a feeling of well-being; it was, in short, marvellous to be in a railway station again and have the money to buy a ticket and get out of this town in which I had spent nearly two years living on my Jewish nerves. Will they get me or not? In the new body of Jan Gerrit Overbeek I felt safe for the first time. It's insane to walk about freely when you are supposed to be sitting in some camp. Insane maybe, but it also makes one contented and happy, to be that insane. Schizophrenia did not hurt for a change. To be schizophrenic is to be normal; unreality is reality. I was both. Overbeek for the world and J. L. for this other world, who might or might not come back when the Germans have lost the war. It wasn't good enough to hate the Germans, it wouldn't do only to despise the Nazis, one also had to be convinced that the Germans will lose and the Allies win. An enemy can only be defeated if we are ready to believe that he must ultimately lose.

I shared the second-class compartment with eight other people; trains always off schedule were always overfull. I gave each one of the people, patriots and Blackshirts (there were two of the Blackshirts in the window seats) a nasty look as a kind of introduction. I didn't look fearless, whatever that is; I just looked disgusted by the very sight of them. For what I recognized as Nazis in civilian garb, I added a drop of wry smile into my expression. Watch out, buster, I said (with looks), I am a bigger Nazi than you. I can hate four times more than you. As a Zionist, as an Austrian, as a left-wing Socialist, and as a Dutchman. And having, as part of my identity kit, an Austrian Aryan mother (in case my Dutch seemed not too perfect to some people), I also despise you as a "real German." I had one or two checkups on the train. They were not looking for me, but for Jews who had not gone to Westerbork and young Dutchmen over eighteen who should be in Germany as slave labour. I was not a Jew and too young for the general call-up. A few weeks later — at my third checkup in the streetcar between Utrecht and Zeist — I had my first slight brush with a German Military Police patrol. One of them reprimanded me in a fatherly way that I should keep my card clean at all times in a special cellophane holder one can buy for a few pennies in any stationery shop. I said I would.

The farmer didn't like me too much, as I didn't know how to milk cows and had been sent to him as a farmhand from the labour exchange. I did my best, but fell asleep constantly. When the quarrels became too hefty, he threatened to send me back to wherever I came from. I had to leave. I didn't much like going back, aware of how hard it was to get a new address. On the other hand, it was dangerous to stay with someone you quarrel with. I wish they had found me an easier job. I never liked to get up at five in the morning and work until dusk, packing hay on a horsecart. Those jobs look much easier when we see them from a train window. My dislike for manual labour had been part of my trouble as a Pioneer. Manual labour was definitely not for me, and farming the most boring existence in the world. A pity they had no office jobs. I would have like to spend my evenings less tired and in female company. Convinced I couldn't stay here for much longer, I wondered where I could go. After Jutphaas where the cows rejected my clumsy attempts to take them at their udders, I couldn't possibly show up again in Amsterdam and ask for another address. They might have thrown me out.

Instead, I was sent by an underground messenger to work as a gardener. I had to do my very best not to break pots, not to step on small seedlings, not to cut the flowers too short. We delivered flowers to the garden across the road. A former seminary for young priests that had turned into a headquarters of the German Naval High Command for the Netherlands.

Being on the right footing with the Germans across the road, Kuperus, for whom I worked, kept two Jews and one young Navy lieutenant under the counter. This way Kuperus, garden architect and important man in the local Resistance, covered himself from inquisitive Dutch Nazis with flowers.

I didn't mind the work as much as the Sunday sermons he preached to his wife, his small sons, and his Jews, and didn't mind the sermons as much as the boredom of rural life. There were a few sort of hot-dog stands in the small town for night life, but I wasn't allowed to leave the garden for town. At night I was locked away in an attic. A tiny attic room behind a false wall. I suffered boredom, became more clumsy at work, and hated my protector and his family. To Piet, who claimed to be from Antwerp (his name is Fuchs, I found out after the war, and he is head of the collection of Hebraica at Amsterdam's University Library), I had nothing to say. He was ten years older, a scholarly, square type, small, with receding dark hair and black eyes. Piet didn't like me much either, I think. He was born in Poland, with Polish as his mother tongue; in short, a Pole, and I was an Austrian. And like all Austrians I couldn't talk to Poles, Czechs, Hungarians — who all are provincials in the eyes of the Viennese — without showing some of my Viennese arrogance, whether I liked it or not. It wasn't a conscious attitude, it came naturally.

Fuchs must have despised me because I was apparently miserable and obviously not appreciating what Kuperus was doing for me. He was not supposed to know that I was anyone but Jan, but like I knew straightaway that his name was not Piet, he must have sensed the truth about me. The other character in the garden under Kuperus was a man of about twenty-four or twenty-five who claimed to have been a Navy officer, but he didn't look like one to me. He called himself Brinkman, looked a bit like Jaap who had lost two packets of cigarettes to me when I proved my manhood in a handkerchief for him.

Brinkman could tell stories like Jaap. He talked only about whorehouses in Amsterdam and Hamburg and what one could learn there. His conversation at length was boring, but for half an hour or so it was entertaining, exciting, and instructive. He was the first who pointed out to me that two girls in bed are better than one. He told me of whipping scenes, of lesbians, of women tied down with ropes. Horrible stories, I thought, and listened with my mouth open, pretending to have seen it all before. I packed out every single fantasy Jaap had told me and added a few little details myself. Brinkman was impressed and so we became friends. But it wasn't a real friendship. He seemed interested only in male and female sex organs; I was also interested in discussing Spinoza and politics.

"Too much thinking is shit, Jan. You don't need to think so much or you will get crazy. Give me anytime a nice juicy cunt and you can keep your philosophers. That's *flauwe kul*." Meaning: a drag. But thinking was all that was left to do between meals and after dark. All there were to read were some old-fashioned bad books, which no one had touched for fifty years, and, of course, the Bible. Kuperus belonged to an Old Testamentarian Protestant sect, the name I don't recall — something like the Church of the Disciples of our Good Lord Jesus.

I sometimes picked up the Bible in my room, just to have something to read, and put it down after a few moments. The monotonus addings up of strange names sent me to sleep. So and so begot so and so was the brother of so and so and the father of someone else. This can go on for page after page and is definitely not profitable reading for young people. One shouldn't read the Bible before the age of forty if one wants to appreciate some of its moral legends. The story that appealed most to me was, of course, the tale of Joseph and the pit. Surrounded by danger, I too seemed not to have a slight chance ever to get out of this hole. The idea of having to sit out the war in Zeist made me restless and bad-tempered. Kuperus thought I had by now been in Zeist long enough; neighbours and the Germans across the road knew me; I could risk living somewhere else. People like Fuchs, who looked Jewish, needed the protection of the attic room just above their place of work more urgently than I did.

Kuperus found me a bed with a woman not far from the garden. A woman with a son of fourteen and a daughter of seventeen. The daughter worked in a factory that manufactured silver cutlery; the mother went out cleaning; the boy was still at school. A simple family, they spoke in a broad accent, and regarded me as someone "better" than themselves, not just a labourer in the garden of Kuperus. I obviously came of better stock, because my Dutch was slow and I pronounced the vowels, just like educated people do. I got on well with the new family. I liked their potatoes mashed with cabbage. What I disliked was the whole family's taking a bath in the same bowl in which they washed potatoes and vegetables. I had a weird sense of cleanliness at the time. I used to wash several times a day and keep my clothes clean and tidy, must have been so contaminated by this sterilized world that within two years had washed away anything Jewish as if it had been an open wound.

Every morning at seven I left the house, walked down two quiet lanes, and reported to Kuperus for work. Work usually meant planting flowers in the headquarters of the Navy. The only other soul I talked to besides Brinkman was a German soldier from Vienna, when he was on duty in his little black-, white-, and red-striped hut at the entrance. He told me about Vienna, which I claimed to know through stories of my mother's, and with that much in common, he confided in me that he had girls all over the place and that the Army was an ideal job for a man who wants to have a lot of women and has a bitchy wife at home. He was fat and middle aged, stared after every girl who came cycling down the lane, and cursed his duty, or he would be after her and under her skirts within minutes. Anton (Call me Toni) liked talking to me, because he had seen straightaway that I was an educated person. I was flattered, knowing that a simple-hearted Viennese in the German Navy must hate the Germans for the same reasons that I hated the German refugee children (because of their godawful kind of German).

It would take Toni years to see the connection between a different, "educated" young man and a Jew. I couldn't discuss Spinoza with him. He would have said: What did you say? Spinach?

But I didn't mind impressing him with my violent argument against the Pope, the Church, and anything Catholic. Most Viennese like that kind of antipapal emotion, being brought up with obligatory "Our Father which art in Heaven" as soon as they enter school. Not only did I know everything about bishops and cardinals and the orgies of nuns and monks (that's real scum — Toni used to say — shaking his head, the real scum. Not the Jews, the Catholics, my friend.) I also knew the first lines of many songs, school rhymes, and limericks. In fact, I got so enthused about the way I seemed to be able to make friends with Viennese, I thought seriously and for a long time of returning to Vienna with the help of the official Labour Exchange. By the very mention of the words Stefansturm, Prater, Kahlenberg, Kärntrerstrasse, and Wachau, we both sighed.

I think I had more in common with Anton than with all the Granaats and Brinkmans. "Vienna remains Vienna" is a Viennese saying, and all it says is: You can change the world and you can send a Viennese into outer space; he will cringe at the words Steffel (the dome of St. Stephen's Cathedral), Prater (the year-round fun fair), and (the wine houses of) Grinzing. Why? Only God knows. It's part of the psychic distance Viennese like to create to their town. "Psychic distance", my dictionary explains, is the "degree of detachment of an individual from the practical significance or appeal of an object."

In August or September of the same year ('43) Badoglio capitulated, Mussolini fled, the Allies landed in Sicily and prepared their invasion of the mainland. Everyone knew the Germans had lost the war, but it was never advisable to say so to strangers. The end was in sight; it was clearly a matter of holding out and surviving, a matter of wait-and-see and keeping one's nerve. I was bored and impatient and didn't quite know what to do with myself, as I didn't dare to write. Writing, making notes, keeping a diary, outlining a story, or jotting down a poem had been my very private way of spending time, as long as I could recall. I had always written something or other. Back in Vienna, in the refugee camp, in Bussum, and in Gouda. But now writing was dangerous. Dutch labourers do not write. I wouldn't have liked anyone to see me writing, nothing more serious than a postcard; every written piece of paper could fill a Gestapo file with my name on it. Writing was something I dreamed to do again in peacetime, something beautiful and pleasant that will only accur when one is allowed to live again. Jan Overbeek is a ghost, a shadow, a piece of printed paper with a fingerprint and a signature. The body and soul of this Overbeek walks in Westerbork among the ugly people and their screaming children and waits for his call to the guillotine.

The end of the war is in sight, people made bets. The optimists put their cigarettes on "No longer than three to four months," the pessimists gave it six. After the ever-increasing bombardments and the intensified partisan action behind the German lines in Russia, Poland and Yugoslavia, the Dutch Resistance, too, multiplied its attacks on German officers and German personnel. Rauter, the henchman, and Seisz-Inquart, the viceroy, had an "excuse" to wage their all-out war against civilians. The dangerous Jews had gone, only a handful of the especially privileged and rich were left; the new danger was coming. from Dutchmen recruited now in their thousands by the Resistance. To grab this potential underground army first, the Germans no longer wished to wait for their "Aryan brothers" to volunteer. The men between eighteen and thirty-five didn't want to go. They went to get them. The same methods were used. Barbed wire to seal off a quarter, loudspeakers to call them out of their homes, search parties to go after them. The lorries that had run the Jews to the theatre and on to Westerbork were now dumping able-bodied men by the thousands on open railway trucks and into river barges, where they forced them at gunpoint into overcrowded holds. Next day the survivors were unloaded. in a private camp of Alfried Krupp, or left to slave in an I. G. Farben subterranean ammunition dump.

It became dangerous to be a male, only cripples or doddering old-aged pensioners were free. Once picked up because you are not supposed to be behind your mother's apron, the screening could be hazardous. If I wanted to go on living, I had to get to Germany myself sooner or later. Preferably sooner than later. The *Razzias* had come to Zeist. Kuperus and his flowers could not cover up for much longer the smell of illegality. "I wish I were a flower, I might outlive this Autumn," I poeted and flushed this bit of written evidence down the toilet.

Why and how Charles appeared just at this time I don't know. Call it fate, coincidence. But he had to come, that's why he came. Charles was the boy friend of the girl in the house. He worked on a river barge, had been a sailor even before the war. Occasionally, once in two months or so, whenever he had a few days off and the ship was moored in Rotterdam, he came to see his sweetheart. He came twice while I was there. The second time on a Saturday he stayed for lunch, took his girl friend to the woods, brought her back for supper, to take her afterwards to a cinema in town. The second time we said "Hello" like old friends. He too looked up to me as someone from the "educated classes." He was probably flattered when I told him that I would like nothing more in the world than to be his helper on the boat. Most of the Dutch river barges had been taken over by German firms like Stinnes and Raab-Karcher and were now sailing under a German flag. The captains were usually Germans, many of them retired old men, who had to serve the fatherland for a second time in twenty-five years. They didn't like this. The old and the crippled in Germany were back at work, the able-bodied men in the occupied countries were exhented to do the same. It's only fair, they said. War is war, we don't like it either.

I didn't have to lie to Charles. Who likes to work for the Germans? I was nearly eighteen and any day they could carry me off. I told him the truth. I prefer working on a barge to sweating in a factory; it seems more interesting than carrying cement bags up the Atlantic wall, and more adventurous than sweating it out on a farm. Charles had one Frenchman on board ("a lazy bastard"). Experience or no experience, a third man was a luxury. The third man does the dirty work, carries provisions on board, prepares the meals, and cleans the cabin, next to his normal duties of painting, cleaning, opening and closing the holds. A third man is always useful and if you can get one, better take him.

"Whatever it's going to be, it won't be dull, Jan." I wanted to leave right away. I had had more than enough of Zeist. I was fed up with Toni, who, every time he saw me, knew another little Viennese ditty I should know if I didn't know it yet, another little joke I might have missed last time he had told it to me; I was tired of Brinkman and his whorehouse fantasies — they didn't let me sleep; and the silent conversations with Piet from Antwerp, staring at each other when we picked flowers or strawberries, I could easily miss out on.

The *Razzias* had come to town. Soon it might mean hiding underneath the strawberries. I saw the *Matthias Stinnes 72* with me at the helm sailing the wide-open seas, cigarette in the corner of my mouth, and the sound of a mouth organ from aft deck. Sailing down to the Cape of Good Hope to load cinnamon and ivory tusks for Bombay. "How do I get on this boat, Charles? Doesn't one need experience? Are you sure the Captain will take me? I have never been on a boat before."

"He will take you, Jan, don't worry. He will take you." And as I still looked worried, Charles added, "if he doesn't, I pack my things and go to another boat. How does that sound to you?" I doubted whether the Captain would mind if Charles went somewhere else, but didn't know that, because of the labour shortage and the German firms' competing for the foreign labour available, he would indeed not wish to lose an experienced sailor to another firm.

A few days later there was a note in the mail. "We are in Rotterdam, Milestone 322, it's the *Matthias Stinnes*, we are opposite the refineries. Everything OK. You can come." I told Kuperus. I needed a passport. The ship would cross several frontiers on its trips — Belgium, Holland, Germany, and maybe even France. I needed a passport or there would be no boat for me in Rotterdam. Kuperus, glad to be rid of one of his protégés, promised a passport, and produced it three days later. I went up to the Town Hall with two passport photographs and signed it.

From my salary (Kuperus paid us regular salaries) I bought myself a new skin. Strong corduroy trousers, a blue turtleneck sweater (eighty points from the ration card for textiles), and a blue seaman's cap (four points). I went to the hairdresser and had my hair cut short, because short hair makes the Aryan; collected two silver rings I had on order, one with the initials of my new love to whom I mailed it via a contact address, with a letter that said: "I am leaving now for Germany and don't know when I will be back. But I will love you forever." (My God, did I love her round behind.) The second ring with "J. O." I wore myself. I said good-bye to everyone, including Toni whom I had to promise to visit after the war in Vienna, and took a train to Rotterdam.

I was in high spirits. The road, my road, did not lead to Spain over the Pyrenees nor to Switzerland via Vichy France; by now I was afraid to go anywhere but to the very heart of the monster. Inside the lion's mouth I would not have to fear the animal's teeth and claws. A prolonged stay in Holland was to provoke the wrath of the gods; to survive the *Götterdämmerung* I had to climb Mount Olympus by myself.

The day I entered Germany on board the *Matthias Stinnes 72*, a 1,400-ton barge, at home in Duisburg, on 2 November 1943, I crossed a meridian into a new self. The small town of Emmerich on the German-Dutch border was the threshold into a new rationality. A madness it looks now. I had waked up — from a sleep called childhood, from a dream called Jewish suffering — into a world of stark facts. The new world was the river. Like all sailors I loved and hated the ship and soon dropped all sentimental affiliation, to Vienna, Jews, Jerusalem and family, overboard. They drifted for a while behind the rudder, a dead dog, and slowly out of sight.

This is the time, sailing under the flag of a false self, to think about "God and the world". Whether washing the boat, cooking a meal, cleaning the cabin, or standing at the wheel, even in the beer houses amongst the deafening noisy people — there is time to "think". Thinking is my freedom to be myself. And what do I think? First of all: This can only happen once in a lifetime, after the war there can never be another one. Secondly: This war will have changed us all. All armies and flags, all medals and fancy hats will go on the same rubbish heap on which the bricks and water pipes, the cutlery and furniture go. After this war this is going to be a new world. It will never be the same again. Never again. This is a great war, after this war is over there will be eternal peace.

What do I think? I think they don't want to face it, and they don't want to face it (defeat) because they know they are evil. I am ready to face them with a forged paper. No one knows who I am. If anyone looks at me, I stare at him so he will look away. What do *they* think, these idiots? I'm not as smart as they are? I know they want me to admit the Jew, wear a yellow patch, and go and die. But I don't want to. I refuse. Go and get me, if you can find me. Is there no one looking for me? No one cares whether you are alive or dead. It hurts. How do I know they don't look for me? Because they don't find me. With all their many smart police and Gestapo officials, hundreds of informers, and a helpful population, they don't find me. Why don't they come and shoot me? They don't want me, they don't care. They. The world. I do not exist.

It is good to be alive while being dead. I think, life is adventurous, dangerous, funny. First of all, it is fun to see new countries. I hadn't seen Belgium before and I had never been to Germany, but had heard a lot about the beautiful Lorelei and dreamy castles in the valley of the Rhine, about the green pastures and vineyards. The black, ugly industrial Ruhrgebiet. Hard, black, rough, soot, smog, fog — weird shapes in the fog, belching fire and smoke — Germany is beautiful. Alight or not. Never knew that I loved fires. Every house alight is one house less. Every dead German one enemy less. The war kills the right people, burns the right houses down (for a change). This is not Rotterdam in 1940 — this is Mannheim being wiped out in '44. Mannheim or Koblenz, Munich or Cologne, Hamburg or Berlin. I think: What does it matter? Every bomb is a good deed. To kill the murderers is doing at least something to liberate the prisoners.

All those people who left with their parcels of sixty pounds each are dying somewhere in a camp — they all would be happy to know, I think, that Germany is being blown up and burned down. It's raining bombs. And everyone can see for himself — bombs are not stuffed with liver sausage. The war is the war is the war. them: wish I could tell them. If I could, I would tell them: Don't worry, people. I would tell them: the Germans are getting killed, their houses are rubbish heaps, their water cut off, gas and coal supply cut off every other day. The housewives grumble, the invalids look sad, the soldiers are tired — everyone is bad-tempered. They drink to forget their trouble. They *are* in trouble. Not much longer, people (I would say if I could), soon it will all be over. They will hang the bastards who now stride around in their big black boots, they'll hang them and shoot them, they will bury them and their country — a heap of rubbish is all that will be left of this pretty countryside — hold out a bit longer, people, the end is near.

How could there be another war after that? I think. What are they going to bomb? When all that's left of a house are two bricks and a chimney pot? How many can they arrest and deport and kill? But talking is impossible. Two words too many and you end up behind bars. They sort you out with the help of thumbscrews; next day you die in a bleak courtyard. The war is on. The end is in sight. But it's not going quickly enough. Wherever there are Germans — in the Balkans, in Greece, in Bosnia, in Poland, in the Ukraine, in France, in Belgium, in Holland, in Denmark, in Norway — wherever there are Germans, there are enemies of these bastards and

the enemies of Germans do not sleep. The papers tell a pack
of lies. Every defeat is twisted into a victory. Successful attacks and counteroffensives are being invented to soothe the
public mind. They can tell it to the Marines.

But I — Jan Gerrit Overbeek — I know the truth. I can see
everything with my very own eyes. I don't have to think, I
can see. I see life and death in pictures — a river, a bridge,
white houses, a few trees, a green meadow, yellow flowers, red
apples, red strawberries. Yellow pictures. Yellow of bread and
cheese. Yellow skin. Yellow nursery. Yellow thoughts. Frightened. Yellow Holland. In Germany the colours are brighter:
pinks, mauve, white, purple — a light violet. German. Bombs.
Boats. Water. Fear. Every house is a bright light or pleasing
colour. Every valley a beautiful valley — every meadow,
river, bridge is beautiful. The rest has gone up in flames.
Home from home. Ukrainians in the beer houses. Sunday.
They wear padded jackets, their boots are made of wood.
Ostarbeiter are marked with an "O" on their backs. Loading,
unloading, working on the railroads, marching in small
groups to a building site, their feet bandaged in rags against
the cold. An old Russian custom. Rags keep the cold out far
better than rabbit-fur-lined paper boots, sold for leather
against coupons. I love the Russians and Ukrainians and
their sad melodies. They are my friends.

And my friends are the drunks, the whores, and the hangers-on, my friends are sailors, soldiers, and carpenters Heinrich is a carpenter, but he doesn't work. They don't want him
in the Army. His lungs are still full of the gas of World War I.
He may die in a few months. Heinrich has two girl friends.
His local is the Anker. In the Anker we all meet. The Anker is
the wildest thing in Duisburg-Bostropp. Heinrich's girl
friends are sixty and twenty. Mutti—everyone calls her that—
is sixty, and Inge is twenty. Heinrich owns them both. But as
he had to go back to his wife for the weekend, Heinrich trusts
me. I may take both women home. Inge is drunk, throws up
all over the floor and the tables and is menstruating. Mutti
can't cope with her tenant all by herself. The two women live
together, because Mutti's son is in the Army and God knows
where. Mutti doesn't like being on her own. We carried Inge
out from the bar; and we carried her up the stairs and put her
to bed. She snores, spits and farts. Mutti went to her room to
wrap up little parcels to send to her son on the *Ostfront*. She

has thousands of things in glasses and tins — strange old lady. She says: Now you go and sleep with Inge, but behave yourself, she is very sick.

I say: Like a gentleman. I go in, the room is full of alcohol fumes; I lie down next to Inge and want to fuck her, but it wouldn't be nice to make a drunken lady; I don't. The next thing — the story went round that I had not made use of Inge; everybody else, of course, would have. I had behaved like a gentleman. I must be mad. It made me very different among the sailors. I was the intellectual among them. I read good books, but hid them. I made entries in my diary and pretended they were letters to a friend. Later I would tear these pages out. A lot of my behaviour could have been suspicious, could have caused me trouble.

Thank God we are never too long in the same place. The boat takes two and no more than three days to load and unload. We carry coal, but sometimes ingot, the iron and steel leftovers from the factories. The Dutchmen know each other and you can trust them for the most part, but it's better to keep one's mouth shut. I might be a bit peculiar among the sailors, like not fucking drunk, sick, and menstruating sluts, but only once did someone joke, in Heilbronn when we had all sat down for an evening of rum, "Jan is just like a Jew. He knows everything." Of course I talked about God and everything, whenever there was the slightest chance to talk about anything but girls.

I got up and socked the boy who wanted to insult me. "That's not a joke." I said, "I hate the fucking Germans, I admit, but don't you call me a Jew."

"But Jews are OK. Don't get angry."

"But I don't like them," I said. He apologized.

Two days later in Mainz I went to a well-known dance hall, which had been the big synagogue before they burnt it down in '38. On one part of a pillar that held up an improvised roof, there was a marble slab with the names of the founders in Hebrew letters. I saw no other traces of these strange people, who had lived along the Rhine for about a thousand years and had vanished into thin air. I too belonged to these strange people; I too was invisible, just like them.

I began to wear my "Gestapo hat" again — the grey one with the rim all the way down, the one I had worn the day I

84

had left after the "earthquake" of June the 20th. With the rim pulled down and the collar of my coat standing on end, I threw the shadow of a criminal, a burglar, on the wall; he may also be a spy or a detective. The kind of shadow that makes you wonder, "Who goes there?" And about the same time as I took to wearing these props that made me a suspect creature to project a shadow of myself against any wall, a poster appeared all over the country. You saw it in shop windows, in shops, in offices, and on railway stations; you saw it (in smaller size) stuck against the windows of streetcars, and carried among the ads on backs of buses. This poster showed the shadow of a man with a rim of his hat down, and the collar of his coat on end. And underneath it said: *Pst. Achtung — Feind hört mit.* (Pst. Careful — the enemy listens in.) It should tell the people not to talk to foreigners and strangers about their place of work, about the damage in town after a bombardment, about the arms and trucks that might have passed on the railway. Don't talk! it says, the enemies of Germany are everywhere.

Two and a half million foreign labourers in the Reich and maybe a few thousand of them voluntarily — there were plenty of enemy ears, and probably many of them excluding me listened for the Resistance, doing espionage and sabotage — but not a single one of these foreigners cast a shadow like mine.

It's then that I knew — on the way back from the Anker through a sleepy town, meeting no one but a few drunks and some policemen, passing hundreds of posters that *wanted* only one man in the entire Reich — that I was invisible. As no one could see in me the man from the poster, no policeman on his beat and no girl behind the bar, no MP's in the ports and no official in the rationing office, I must have disappeared totally. At the time it didn't occur to me that I looked just my age. Seventeen. Seventeen maybe to the world, my real age had doubled. J. L. was seventeen. J. O. was eighteen. In 1944 I was thirty-five years old, which makes me fifty-eight now. Not surprising I feel young when my present passport tells me I was born in '27.

Not really. I was born sometime in June '44. In Ludwigshafen. We had just tied her down, lying deep in the water with coal. It was lunchtime. The alarm seemed like a whistle for lunch break. You could see them against the light blue sky, against the sun. Tiny silver wings fluttered high up in the heavens. A thousand of them. Maybe more. Who can count them? They come whenever they like. There is no Luftwaffe. Göring, who promised he would call himself Mayer (a German way of self-humiliation) if ever an Allied plane would cross over Germany, had not a single Piper Cub to send up. Whenever they decide, they come. If you see wings fluttering under God's throne, there is usually no reason for alarm, let them howl hysterically. This time it was different. Nothing seemed to fall from above. The earth itself exploded. We, Theo and I (it's the *Hugo Stinnes 30* I am on), were ready for lunch. I prepared smoked sausage with the *stamppot* (potatoes mashed with cabbage), a special treat. It's a year ago I left Retiefstraat, time to celebrate. We have three bottles of wine, three large bottles, straight from a cellar in Nierenstein, cheap. Ready for our party — and the earth explodes. I get up to go ashore, prepared to jump overboard if necessary. Theo doesn't want to move.

"Shit, Jan, stay where you are."

"You stay where you are." And faster than a cat chasing its prey, I jump across three barges, balance like a goat over a cliff, nearly break my neck over a steel rope, and I am ashore. The day of justice has come. The earth opens up to swallow all that breathes. There is nowhere to run. I slide down a new crater, maybe eight or ten feet deep. The earth is dry, yellow, not a drop of water. I lie inside the volcano (no two bombs fall on the same place is the legend). I lie there and can hardly hear the explosions, I am too deep down below, I can't see anything but the inside of the newly shovelled grave. I am safe with mother, I am in her belly — I and a little insect that is climbing up a stone, thinking it's the Himalayas, are the only survivors. I can hear birds. Very loud, very hectic and nearby.

I climb slowly up to see some more of this world. Two, three more explosions. Then total silence. I. G. Farben is burning, people run in all directions. There are ships in mid-river, a train passes a bridge. There are ships moving upstream and downstream. But of the *Hugo Stinnes 30* there is only the rear end left, and the two boats next to it seem to be sinking. What did happen in these forty-five minutes? A long high-pitched sound, like someone shrieking down my ear. End of alarm. A new rebirth in June '44. I am lucky. Imagine! ... and can't imagine it. I am alive and want to wash my hands. I am alive and hungry and regret the sausage and the wine and the lunch that has gone to the fishes. Together with Theo and a few of his friends they will enjoy it.

This kind of therapy, the apocalyptic kind, cures one of many pains. I was hungry and stretched myself in the grass, lit a cigarette and thought, "That's that". Once the earth has opened beneath you and you walk out of your grave, you fly higher than American Fortresses. You stay up. Ludwigshafen and Mannheim are burning. One has to see the positive side of it all. I left the womb in Ludwigshafen in June '44, that makes me twenty-four now. Not surprising I feel old when I look at my passport and see 1927. In Ludwigshafen, in Mannheim, in Heilbronn and in Duisburg, in Leverkusen and Herne and in another dozen towns I was born and reborn, at least twice a week.

"Charles was killed and Theo was dead and I took myself north to Duisburg," to find another boat. The *Matthias Stinnes 18*. She was not such a good boat as the previous ones. The cabin was damp and rotten, the stove far too large, leaving no space for a small table, two chairs, a double bunk, and two young men. The skipper was an old man of probably seventy-five from Heidelberg. His name was Bacher. His wife was not much younger. The only cheerful sight in this family was their daughter in her mid-twenties, who occasionally stayed on board for a few days. Bacher, whose hands were constantly trembling, was a loud-mouthed, angry old man, who wouldn't let a sentence pass without the word *Scheisse*, in spite of the fact that his wife reminded him with a reproachful "But, Eduard, is that necessary?" It certainly was necessary. On the 20th of July and the arrest of the generals, Bacher had taken gleefully the official line and cursed "these gangsters who want to stab the Reich in the back."

After this kind of remark I decided that it was time that I started my private war of sabotage against the Reich, no matter what the consequences would be, with a go-slow. "Lift your feet you *Scheisskerl*, you *Scheissholländer*, a little quicker you *Arschloch*, you *Holländischer Schweinehund*." (Little did he know that I was a *Saujude* as well. Had he known that, he would have pushed me overboard with his own hands, knowing that I couldn't swim.)

Our quarrels never ended. And as the war went better for

us, I got more self-confident and once let myself go to say the most humiliating thing one can ever say to a German: "Leck mich am arsch," meaning "lick my arse." Unlike the rest of the world, the Germans have no use for the expressive term "fucking". The word "fucking" can only be used when it means just that. What is considered dirty and therefore insulting by the Anglo-Saxons means nothing to the Germans. For them, everything that has to do with the rear end, faeces, and the anus is real filth. That's why the words *Arsch, Scheisse, Arschloch*, and "Lick my arse" are "real and serious insults"; they can only be used by people according to hierarchy.

Insult is the privilege of the powerful. A director, a boss, an officer, a captain can call those underneath his rank any name he fancies; but saying to your superior "Lick my arse" is equivalent to patricide. A revolution against the crumbling Hitler Reich with a go-slow (it wasn't all that conscious — half the time I was really more or less asleep); my "Lick my arse" addressed to Bacher was an obvious provocation addressed to Berlin. Lick my arse, Hitler, Goebbels, and Göring, lick my arse, Himmler, Rauter, and Seisz-Inquart, I am a Dutch labourer, my name is Overbeek, I came here voluntarily to help (myself). The first part of this sentence and the last word I kept to myself when I had to repeat in front of two civilian policemen (usually referred to as Gestapo) what I had said to the skipper. I had used this insult of all insults against such a high authority. "I am a Dutch labourer, my name is Overbeek," I repeated. "I came here voluntarily to help and the skipper never leaves me in peace with his constant shouting at me. I can't help it if I'm not as fast as my mate Klaas who is a professional sailor; I can only do my best." The Germans (like Russians) love confessions.

I had to promise to mend my ways or learn how people are doing in a *Straflager* (a punishment camp). Buchenwald, Dachau, Oranienburg, Auschwitz had their special *Straflager* attached to them, in case anyone might try his luck to survive gas chambers and executions. I didn't know about the gas chambers, but exactly like the rest of the public I knew a *Straflager* is a hole in the ground if you are fortunate. I didn't mend my ways. I left the Gestapo at the lock at Herne with the wild intention of increasing my war against Bacher and his fatherland by going even slower, though I would not beg him again to lick my arse, after all the *Scheisse* he had slung at me.

The method worked more or less. The skipper didn't really want to lose me, because Klaas, the first mate, would kick up a fuss if he had to run the boat alone with an eighty-year-old couple. So somehow all went well for a while after the interrogation. I had girls on my mind. Couldn't find enough of them — we never stayed long enough in a place. The girls in the bars were usually professionals and there was a strong chance of getting coshed over the head and robbed during operations. The other girls one could meet — shop assistants, office girls in shabby dance halls or in the street — were even more a risk. Syphilis and gonorrhoea (a knight's illness the Germans called "the clap" for some obscure reason) were widespread. It was healthier to stay home and masturbate. But masturbation made me tired and bad-tempered.

My mind was on girls and how to find them. How to find them first and how to find a place to take them to. The girls usually lived with their parents. I had no money and no inclination to take them to a hotel. Checking in and out of hotels I didn't care for. The abodes of love were bombed-out houses, patches of grass between two factory walls, an abandoned junkyard, the wall of an asylum for stray dogs at the edge of a town.

I was seventeen — I wanted and needed a girl friend. I found one in Frankfurt-on-the-Main. Her name was Natasha, which made her Russian, Ukrainian to be exact, from Kiev. Because she was pretty and maybe better educated, but probably because she looked like any other pretty German girl with blue eyes and dark hair, she had been privileged to work in a household instead of in the factory where she had been for a year. I even believe Natasha was Jewish, she had Jewish eyes; I never discussed it with her. She walked the dog, a big wolf he looked to me, not far from where she worked. Prowling for girls, I said something to her and she smiled back. We walked through a little park, sat on a bench together, I looked into her eyes, found something there that looked pleasant and familiar, and was ready to follow her to the end of the world. (There was a thirty-kilometre boundary around every town for foreigners unless the police and the labour exchange gave you special travel permission).

89

I don't know whether I wanted to marry her the first day in the park; I certainly promised her I would, as soon as the war would be over. I figured she, being Russian, was the solid type of girl who might see nothing wrong in making it with her fiancé. For the time being we agreed to meet again a week later. We were staying in Frankfurt's Osthafen for at least two weeks, as the ship needed some repairs.

Three days later the little silver angels practically sank the entire Osthafen. The town was burning from one end to the next. Our ship was not touched. I counted the hours until Thursday. Thursday at two at the same spot in the park. Opposite a little-used air-aid shelter, another place for making love, if there are no bombers over the town. The air-raid shelter is the place it is going to happen. I knew that, though I wasn't quite sure what we were going to do with the wolf. To look really at my best for this date (Natasha was far prettier than my Dutch girl friend; I consequently loved her more already), I planned to buy myself a new pair of shoes for which I had coupons and money but no time so far to choose them. Before the shops would close I went to town. Six shoe shops I walked out of, they only carried black shoes. Brown shoes are not the fashion, they said. But I wanted brown shoes, fashion or no fashion. Black shoes depressed me, I didn't want to have anything black on me. The seventh shop had the colour I wanted but not the exact size. One size smaller.

"Too small" was the verdict of the salesgirls.

"But I'll buy them."

"They will hurt," the girls suggested.

"I don't feel it," I said. I would rather have gone to see Natasha without a shirt and tie than in black shoes. Black shoes would have discoloured for me the blue of her Volga eyes. Brown shoes. I put them on. I had only three-quarters of an hour left and half an hour's walk ahead. It was a main thoroughfare with trees and benches, or I would never have made it. On every bench I had to sit down to take off the shoes and rub my feet. I was sure that I would never make it. It was ten to two, I was going to be at least five minutes late. The last five minutes were wading through Dante's hell. The brown shoes were made of white hot iron and not of wood and sackcloth.

Natasha and the wolf were waiting. I didn't want to bother

her with my suffering, that's the kind of Continental gentleman I was, and we talked about Kiev and Amsterdam. I turned poet and recited her one of the worst poems ever written, but Russian girls appreciate boy friends who recite poems for them. I knew that, because she listened to anything I said with the kind of eyes reserved for music halls and theatres. She stroked me with her eyes when I quoted from memory: (I still have it, it's dated 27 October 1941.)

A dance of shadows up and down,
dead flowers on your grave,
that's life.

You think yourself a giant,
fate grips you
and throws you down.

No cock crows for you,
no dog barks.
The world goes on and on on giant wheels.

And as she liked that, poor girl, I recited the cheerful rhyme (dated 16 October 1941, thank God, or I could never reprint it):

Don't lose courage
forget the torture,
even as the sun sets
the sun shines.

She kissed me gently on the cheek for these conspiratory words. "Do not give up hope, the war will soon be over," this rhyme really said. She understood. We practically touched hands when we walked into the shelter. The dog we tied to the entrance. But even on top of the bunk, filled with straw, I didn't dare take my shoes off as we might have to leave suddenly. I didn't manage to find time to unbutton. We were both seventeen; at seventeen no garment needs to be removed. Love is strong enough to make any material transparent. As it was getting on to three, when she had to be back, we only had time left to exchange passport photographs, but not for a second time that might have relieved my agony for a

91

few seconds. My feet didn't want to die off, they went on hurting in waves of rising and falling sufferability. I was sad and glad to leave Natasha, and as soon as she was out of sight I took my shoes off and walked back in socks. It was like gliding over clouds in a dream, a hundred times better than fucking.

We stayed a week longer than anticipated in Frankfurt, but Natasha and her dog had vanished. I spent many hours in my worn old shoes in the little park, but she must have had enough of this Dutch poet, which I could hardly believe. That's why I rather assume that her *Hausfrau* must have been watching us from the window, last time, and decided to send her to another park and another poet.

On one of my walks back from these imaginary dates in the park I went to a movie house in the old centre of town. *Die Goldene Stadt (The Golden City)* with the Elizabeth Taylor of the Reich — Kristina Söderbaum. A romantic tale of love and heartbreak set in Prague (the golden city). Not in the Prague of Heydrich and massacres but in the Prague of our Emperor Franz Josef. A safe distance. The Empire was a time (as everybody believes) without politics. Another time I went to see Hans Holt, the Gregory Peck of the Reich, in the wig of Wolfgang Amadeus Mozart, who, after a hectic life of playing the piano and conducting a court orchestra, dies of consumption in a badly lit room, worn out, tired, indebted to everyone, and in love with his sister-in-law. He died young because the title *Whom the Gods Love (Wen die Götter lieben)* had to be justified. I boycotted political films like *Hitler Junge Quex* and *Jud Süss*, and while I decided that Mozart's music (I went to see the movie twice because of the music) was not responsible for what happened in Austria after '38, I had my doubts about it. The theatres played Schiller, Goethe, and Kleist, and the concert halls advertised Beethoven, Mozart, and Bach. They had dropped Mendelssohn and Mahler from their repertoire — they could do without Jewish composers. The German KULTUR and the "new order" of the Nazis had obviously a lot more in common with each other than with people like Mendelssohn and Meyerbeer. Beethoven's and Wagner's music, of course, sounded well in the New Heroic Germany, but Bach and Mozart, Telemann and Schubert were not out of time and place either. Classical German culture agrees with any kind of politics. There was a place for all of it: Streicher and *Fidelio,* Bach and my skipper, Bacher. One could go on freely associating with names like Kiesinger and Lübke, Strauss and Schröder. In fact everything German fitted as in a puzzle. Names like Brandt and Ulbricht, and many thousands of others whose names I do not know, were the exceptions.

Apart from the bombardments that caused certain disruptions in traffic and quite a few housing problems, and apart from the very small minority who did something against this regime, life went on normally for me. I had a job and my monthly salary and waited for the end, just like everybody else. The Allies had landed in France, Italy was practically lost, and the building sites crowded with freezing Italian prisoners in tattered uniforms. Most people looked shabbily dressed and depressed, the foreigners only a bit more so. The food rations for the Germans and for us, because of "heavy work", were agreeable. No one starved. The shops were well stocked, though not with luxuries. The housewives had food stolen from the occupied countries for them and a supply of household help to choose from in an army of foreigners. They were grumbling, but not too loudly, they looked miserable, though not more miserable than now, and said, "War is war." They were just ordinary citizens who worried about themselves and mouthed anything that was opportune. I was one of them. Like most of them I didn't take up arms, did not fight in the Resistance, did not hide anyone in my cabin, apart from one slut whom I had picked up in the Krug in Heilbronn, and that only for one night. And this one single night in the straw with a fat German girl of about twenty changed the further course of my movements. Fate or coincidence? The Latin name for it is *gonorrhoeae,* a venereal disease requiring the exposition of a jealously guarded, circumcised secret. I made a little poem (I translate freely):

All he needed was a foreskin,
otherwise he felt all right.

He lived it up like a Duke on his castle,
with pheasant shooting and old paintings,
all he needed was a little foreskin,
otherwise he was all right.

He lived it up like the Roi de Soleil
on Trianon, they fed him oysters with a spoon,
all he needed was a bit of skin,
otherwise he was all right.

He lived it up like Zeus in the Parthenon,
makes it only with Goddesses,
all he needs is a bit more skin
and everything will be fine.

1. EXISTENCE. If there has been one thing that has
clearly been brought out by the latest advances in physics, it is
that in our experience there are spheres or levels of different
kinds in the unity of nature, each of them distinguished by
the dominance of certain factors which are imperceptible or
negligible in a neighbouring sphere or on an adjacent level,
observes Pierre Teilhard de Chardin in *The Phenomenon of
Man*. Physicists might well conclude that my very special
peculiar existence in the flea-ridden straw of the *Matthias
Stinnes 18* is a natural phenomenon. I didn't think so at
the time. I thought I had fallen out of all spheres and beyond and underneath all levels. I was not part of humanity. I
didn't think so. I am not speaking of loneliness and isolation,
I am speaking of nonexistence. I was and I was not. The *co-
gito ergo sum* I would have replaced with a *Je suis et je ne suis
pas*. Not because my initials had changed and I listened to
another name; my consciousness had ceased to function alto-
ghether. I thought *I knew* what I was doing, on reflection I
know: I did everything by intuition.

Whenever death struck near, I jumped to life, just like I
had done in Ludwigshafen. Wherever I went there was a
downpour of bombs. My very appearance called Marshal
Harris's squadrons out. I was a superagent, whose very brain
concealed a superintelligence device sending radio waves to
the Allied High Command. This mad fantasy was my existence, though I doubted at times whether the device in the
back of my head could go on functioning with such superior,
ingenious perfection forever. No one arrests me. Bombs fall
behind, in front, or a few feet away from me. Not a single
splinter ever hits. The same with the Spitfires. Every day
once or twice they swoop down over the river to machine-gun,

for the heck of it, anything in sight. Quite a number of people were killed or wounded, but the bullets splashed past me into the muddy Rhine. And not only the air protects me against explosives, my own madness shelters me against any slip of tongue. I quarrel with German and Dutch Nazis, with conservative Catholics, rabid anti-Semites and insist that they admit that *not all* Jews should be condemned. "How can an entire people be bad?" and walk away with some sick satisfaction that a stupid man admits to some of his stupidity.

While the pictures of dives, people, and factories fade, while I can no longer refurbish some of the things that went on in the Reich in 1944 — I am not a political correspondent — while every day's life was a dreary routine of washing the boat, "splitting" ropes, cleaning out holds and making meals, buying provisions from little boats along starboard; while all this goes on during the day, and the evenings are spent in the nearest *Gasthaus* among sailors, locals, and girls, something goes on underneath that may have taken only minutes to crystallize but has never dissolved. The feeling that I am something or someone special. Out of all worlds, a world of my own. I have to survive to see the capitulation, because my existence has a purpose. I have to, I said, I have to, no matter what happens. I must live to see the end, and that's why I will see the end. All seemed to me a matter of willpower. I had both. I had my will to make my decisions and the power to carry them out. I didn't want to go on 20 June '43, and that's why I didn't; I wanted to go and hide in Germany and that's why I did. I want to be on a boat as long as all goes well, and that's why I'm on this boat. I soon will want to leave, because it's getting too dangerous on the water and I can't swim, and I'll leave the boat and find something else.

No, I didn't want to get the clap from a slut in Heilbronn, yet I got it. My intuitive reaction to the yellow pus: It's good, it's all right. It hurts and I am frightened but it's all right. I must have wanted it whether I knew it or not. "The little illness" was the obvious way out of a precarious situation. If the main bridge of Cologne which we had to pass on the way to Duisburg had not been bombed a day or two before, I may not have gone first to the small hospital in Boppard near Bonn, but to a bigger one in Duisburg. Once I had set eyes on this comfortable, warm house in Boppard, I decided: This is the right place for coming winter months. A warm room in a sleepy town. I wanted to be a hospital patient, that's why I told the skipper I have syphilis and need at least a month or two to recover. I told the doctor at the hospital that the skipper has no work for me right now, as the boats can't move until they clear away the bridge.

Before I even entered the hospital for the first checkup, I decided: Many non-Jews are circumcised because of dirt that can collect itself under the foreskin and cause an inflammation. It may make me look different from other men, but I am not ashamed of it. It wasn't my fault. That's the way I put it to a male nurse a week later, a pale man of about forty, who treated me with permanganate, a purple liquid better known as a gargle against a sore throat. While he handled my penis, inserting a kind of pump, causing me agony with this internal douche, I joked, "Look at that, they nearly cut it off and now you torture what's left."

"Never mind," he laughed, "it's very common. We'll cure you soon." Giving me another fill of purple poison until I screamed (I let him have his little sadist pleasure,) he added, "That will teach you to put it into every hole that comes along."

"But that's nice," I whimpered.

"Very nice, yes, very nice. (He could see I was perspiring with pain.) Tomorrow I will give you another nice little lesson to look after your tool better."

I hated the treatments and loved the nuns and the food. I was tired and slept most of the day, pretending to be more weak, shocked and upset than any patient in the entire house. Meanwhile it was September or October. The tide had come in. Poland and France were liberated. German civilians handled their foreigners with a shrewd eye on the advancing Allies. It might be a good point in favour to have "always been kind and helpful" to the "poor foreigner." Every bomb that fell increased their respect for power. Real power. A woman in a grocery store in Boppard said to me, "I am glad they bomb us, serves us right. Otherwise we would never understand what we have done to others, and the idiots will go on fighting forever." I dedicate this sentence to the late Winston Churchill, to Bomber Harris, and to all the flying personnel of the Allied air forces. The Allied bombers were the doves of peace. The bombs and only the bombs destroyed the arrogance of the burgher who had believed for far too long

96

that one can get away with murder. Nothing in the history of modern Germany equalled this catharsis straight from heaven; it made West Germany more democratic than it has ever been, and more pacifist than anyone can recall. It needed a large amount of TNT to explode the myth of Teutonic superman and no one ever did more than the pilots and gunners of the Allied air forces to de-Nazify Germany. Only *their* machines could match the cold-blooded mechanized madness called National Socialism.

After a week I went back to the boat to collect all my belongings. I was going to sit out the war in some hospital. Any hospital. From Boppard they moved me to Koblenz. Though I missed half the treatment to delay my discharge, I was, of course, well enough to walk around in town. No one really cared. The country was dissolving, the fanatics in the minority. (The attitude to foreigners changed with the fronts.) After the Städtische Krankenhaus was more or less destroyed (I'd lost all my things and this time even myblack boots), I got the paper that got me coupons to buy myself new clothes. With a friendly smile, I received train tickets and a letter requesting admittance and went one hospital farther.

Two weeks later in Giessen, thanks probably to my special homing device for Allied bombers, the entire town (which had never had a single air-raid all these years) was heavily damaged. This was the evening I had first spent inside the shelter with twenty-two children, two nuns, and a Frenchman. He and I moved to the entrance to "see" what was going on. The shelter and all the other shelters in the hospital garden were ironed out; the building a torch. People screamed for help. Hands were urgently needed to carry those who couldn't walk to safety. And if I hadn't seen, in a dark corridor, the death-skull on a green uniform of this man on a stretcher, I might have pushed a legless human being a bit farther. But I couldn't help a German, and certainly not a German in the uniform of the SS. I wished them all dead and not alive. My war was not over yet.

The war was not yet over. The world around you, still your enemy. If they scream for help, pretend you are deaf; if they want your strength, walk away; if they depend on your sympathy, you have nothing but hate. I realized, before I knew what happened, that life is not only a matter of survival of the body. My compassion for all human beings has ceased to be the essence, the humour, of my life. Squeezed out of its shell, the mind leaves the body and you die with him whom you wish dead. The bombs had been my constant birth and rebirth, the man in the green uniform on a stretcher killed me (and maybe himself) with the magic of a death-skull. He might have been the only man I wilfully killed. Had I done it with a gun in my hand, I might not have died myself. But there it was. The same night Giessen vanished and only a small piece of cement the size of a thumbnail fell on my head, I was killed in an air raid. It took me twenty-five years to find this out. We are all survivors of World War III and II and I. We all exist by miracle or coincident. Death too can be a way of life. The human condition is to let others die and go on *as if* nothing had happened, the *as if* that accepts such a condition is the human part of it. I walked away from the stretcher: The time had come for me as well. I was neither rhinoceros nor sheep. I too was human and therefore mortal. Had I been animal or man from outer space I might have gone on believing in my supermagic powers to survive all wars. After my death in Giessen I had no fear left. I lost it to a legless SS man in the dark corridors of the mind.

I have arrived at the station before the last, Marburg. Again I saw no way ahead and no way back to the boat. Again something had to happen, the hospital was not going to keep me forever. Not a single *gonokokkus* was left inside my urinal tract, however much I beseeched doctors and laboratory assistants to find one under the microscope. I couldn't possibly be cured. It still hurts, Doctor, it hurts. What really hurt was the approaching discharge from the University Clinic Hospital. Sitting in coffeehouses all day long with books and newspapers, and striking up friendships with all sort of locals, German and foreign, did not hurt.

It was already December '44 and the fighting still as fierce as ever. There was no capitulation in sight. Hitler was ready to bury every single German together with himself, and plenty of Germans were ready to die with Hitler. Only a few weeks previously I had seen a hall full of sick people, listening to the Goebbels speech after the offensive in the Ardennes, promising Paris and Brussels back. The crowd was ready to believe him. They folded their faces in the pious, good, National and Socialist citizen look, and bellowed "Heil Hitler" three times as if they were standing high in their boots at a Nuremberg rally and not on their last legs in a peaceful little hospital. Marburg, larger than Boppard, had its Nazis *Sieg-Heil!*-ing behind their radio sets; in the coffeehouse Die Wespe (The Wasp) the only noise was the turning over of the pages and the clanking of little coffee spoons against cups. The housewives and the war invalids, students and office girls had their coffee and cake. I studied Latin grammar and the history of the Roman Empire. I had bought the books for 4 marks at the University bookshop. I would have loved to be a student among other students. They carried books under their arms like bunches of flowers. The prettiest girls collected around them. I was jealous of the peace in which they lived, surrounded by books and pretty girls.

The German Empire was disintegrating faster than any empire before it. I was its historian — a student of history myself. After my death in Giessen I was no longer scared, and made notes continuously; just as a little matter of precaution I headed every new entry in the diary with "Dearest Sweetheart" or something of this sort. I was going to hand the collected letters to Cilly after all was over. Rereading them now (some of it I will reprint later on), I find they are trite bits of writing, but never mind. Another seventeen-year-old "student of history" might not have done so much better.

I slept in the clinic and spent my days in the Wespe brooding about after the war and not quite certain how I was going to make quite sure that I will see its end. I had absolutely no idea. Officially I was on sick leave from the firm of Matthias Stinnes, but sooner or later I would have to report back for duty whether there were a Duisberg and a ship left or not. To take a room in Marburg was unthinkable. I had no permission to live in this town and no intention of going to the Labour Exchange which might pack me off to God knows where. I knew no one in Germany well enough to ask for help. I might have forced some contacts to some sort of Resistance group among the foreigners, but didn't trust any of them and they probably didn't trust me. I had hardly any money left after the purchase of a new suit (as a "student" I had to dress better), but enough for coffee as long as I could take my meals in the hospital. I thought of making my way to the liberated part of Holland. It would mean crossing front lines and too many checkups on the road to the front. I dismissed this adventure as too risky. In short, I needed another miracle to deliver me. I needed someone to take interest in me, someone who had a job for me and would arrange board and shelter and the permission of the Labour Exchange. I needed a new employer. But I had no skills, no training, no school, I was useless. If you don't want to be punished for possessing four Jewish grandparents, you'd better work. Anything will do. Anyone ready to employ me was a good employer.

His name was Kolberg. A Prussian from a Prussian officer's family at Halle an der Saale. Ex-pilot instructor now in charge of a metallurgical research program on behalf of the Air Ministry. His immediate superior is Generalfeldmarschall Milch. We met, standing in a line for a last medical checkup. He was in the Internal Ward, I was in the Skin Ward.

Who are you?

My name is Overbeek. I am Dutch.

What's wrong with you?

Oh, nothing, well something, but it's really nothing.

In which ward?

I forgot.

Come on, in which ward?

Over there. I think it's called Skin Diseases.

Oh. (Little break.) (Of course, he must know.) Where do you work?

I don't work. Used to work on a boat. The *Matthias Stinnes 18* from Duisburg.

Why aren't you there anymore?

I am still with them, but I am on sick leave.

When are they going to discharge you?

Any day. Maybe today.

What are you going to do then?

Go back, I suppose.

Well, are you going back or aren't you?

I don't want to, but I'll have to.

Don't you like it on the boat?

No. Not any more, it's too dangerous.

Why?

Air raids and Spitfires all the time.

What are you going to do if you are not going back to the boat?

I wish I knew.

(A little break and we move along the queue.)

Don't you like it here?

What, here in the hospital? Yes I do, it's all right.

I mean in Germany? Don't you like it in our country?

No. I wish I could go home.

That will take some time.

I suppose so.

Why don't you like Germany?

I am a Dutchman. I don't want to be here.

How come you speak German so well?

My mother is Austrian. Came as a refugee after World War I to Holland, like a lot of Austrians.

So what do you think?

The war is nearly over. The air raids destroy all of Germany. I am not surprised.

Why not?

You are getting it back for what you did to Rotterdam.

You love Holland, right?

Yes I do, and I wish I could go home.

What are you going to do next?

I don't know. I told you. I could go back to Duisburg, but I don't want to. I am sure something will pop up.

Which ward are you in?

The ward for skin diseases.

And what's your name again?

Overbeek, Jan.

What do you do all day?

I read.

You like books?

Yes, I like books.

Have you read Nietzsche?

No, but I have heard of him. Friedrich Nietzsche was a German philosopher who died at the beginning of the century in a Swiss lunatic asylum.

That's right. I will bring you a book by Nietzsche before I leave, maybe today or tomorrow. And inside the book you will find a piece of paper with my address. After they discharge you here, report to me in Dillenburg. We'll see what we can do for you.

Thank you very much.

Good-bye.

I shook his firm hand. He had short, dark hair, a rather handsome face. Brown eyes and a fairly short, slightly dented-in or turned-up nose. Next day, in the afternoon, he came dressed like the director of a big firm and brought me *Thus Spake Zarathustra*. He wore a dark blue suit, white shirt, and black tie. "Get better soon," he said, left the book, and was gone.

I had a long night to brood over it. Shall I go, shall I not go? The note in the book, on a postcard-sized piece of paper, said: "T. Kolberg, Baracke Mittelfeld, Dillenburg/Lahn." To start with, I didn't know where Dillenburg was. But it couldn't be too far. Marburg was on the same river, the Lahn.

I asked someone in the ward. "Dillenburg is about twenty kilometres from here, a small town. Are you going there?"

"Yes," I said, "as soon as I get my discharge." And in this way I suddenly made up my mind. By deciding on the spur of the moment what had kept me awake for a night: In fact, I have nothing to lose.

I arrived in Dillenburg two days later, with my small suitcase, by bus. The train connection was not too reliable. Near the railway station I asked a passerby, showing him my piece of paper, for the Baracke Mittelfeld. "Up there," he said, "up this street, and up the hill, and halfway up to the castle on the right. I think that's the Baracke Mittelfeld. God knows what they are doing up there."

It sounded like a military establishment and it was. The Baracke Mittelfeld was an office of the Air Ministry, evacuated from Berlin. On Dillenburg no one would waste a single bomb. There was absolutely nothing to bomb there. Nothing but one main street, the tiny hotel, the Schwan at the railway station, two or three shops, and a few throughfares. The rest was meadows, trees, and a castle on top of a hill. A sleepy German village in the Westerwald, or not far from the Westerwald; the nearest big town was Wetzlar. I met with new fate, a totally unknown situation, and was told by Fräulein Blom, the secretary of the boss, that Kolberg was away in Berlin, that he had left a message that I might arrive, that I was to stay and wait for him until he came back from his trip, and that I could have an advance in case I was short of money.

It didn't sound too good to be true, because it wasn't true anyway. It was a dream. Fräulein Blom had even arranged quarters for the night, in a villa near the Baracke, the house of a rather well-to-do family. The husband was in the SS and so were her two sons. Their pictures stared at me from a cupboard in the living room. I had a very warm, very clean room overlooking part of the hill. The Baracke itself was out of sight. I had coffee in the morning with fresh rolls and a bath in a real bathtub, and though I walked around as a student of history, I still was the barge sailor. I had felt more at home among the drunks and tarts of the Anker and the Krug than in this house of a solid, respectable SS man.

I wanted to move. I don't like it there, Fräulein Blom. Couldn't you get me another room in the Schwan? She got me a room in the Schwan after two nights. Not having accepted any advance, I felt free to move into other quarters. The room in the Schwan was as simple as a room can be in a village hotel. I immediately felt better. German housewives and tramping Jews don't get on. The pictures of her handsome SS family disturbed me less (or more?) than the creepy clean silence in the house. You felt that even breathing might have upset the arrangement of molecules in the muffy air. Germans quite often have this mortuary atmosphere at home. The rest of the world must indeed look to them like a pigsty in dire need of cleaning up. The Schwan showed a resemblance to normal life. Under the bed and in the corners of the corridors there were still traces of filthy, dirty humanity. The toilets were allowed to stink, and the jackets of the waiters were not impeccably white.

My job was undefinable. He said: Just be around. If I need you, I'll call.

So I sat around, not far from the typists, two fairly pretty young girls, and waited to be called. I preferred the taller one of the two. Let's call her Stella. She was from Dresden. We got on well. The Baracke was four or five large rooms and some smaller ones. The letterhead on the stationery spelled *"Metallurgisches Forschungsinstitut des Reichluftfahrtministerium,"* and Kolberg's letterhead said *"Der Treuhänder des*

Metallurgischen Forschungsinstitutes des Reichsluftfahrtministeriums." A mouthful of German obscurity. I had not the faintest idea what they were doing here. I couldn't make sense, either, from the letters Stella and her friend Lotte typed. Having metals tested for use in the manufacture of airplanes, Kolberg once mentioned. But it sounded a bit weird to me to test metals for planes at this late stage in the war, when they will soon need white flags as their last bit of defence. What planes? Are they still building planes? Who can tell? They were firing rockets to England, the V-1, and a few weeks later the V-2. Jubilation in the local newspapers and on the radio every time they hit a house or a factory in London. The offensive in the Ardennes seemed to have run into difficulties. Too much snow, not enough firepower, not enough soldiers, too many Americans, French, and British against them. The war was practically over. Whom do they try to fool?

Well, Kolberg tried to fool me into believing that his job, and the job of his scientists on the staff (there were about four or five gentlemen in white coats walking in and out of offices), was to test the strength and durability of metals for imaginary Messerschmitts. I didn't know what they were up to and didn't care too much either. Having carried stones for the Atlantic Wall on the boats and coal for Krupp's guns, I might as well help testing metals to put in Messerschmitts. It's all finished for them anyway, and besides, I wasn't much of a help. Just sitting around and writing a few addresses, filing away blueprints, helping the old couple of retainers and a French POW sawing wood for the stoves. Much help I was. I was a bit impatient and disapointed. It looked like a place that had interesting jobs to hand out, but none for the ex-barge sailor from Holland. All the same I was on the payroll. Officially called "Private Assistant to Mr. Kolberg," I drew something like 400 marks monthly from the money Kolberg got from Göring and Milch to spend on his private Jew.

I already had my envelope with the first salary and owed the personnel manager, a fat man of about fifty, a curriculum vitae. A matter of formality every employee of the Ministry had had to submit. I got a typewriter, moved it near the stove, lit a cigarette, and went to town on a short outline of my life.

"One page is enough," the personnel manager had told me. "Red tape requires it. What can you do?"

Since I was Kolberg's favourite, the rest of the staff treated me with a certain respect. They didn't know either why I was around. Consequently, there must be a good reason for it. I thought the same. Kolberg obviously has something in mind if he wants to keep me here and doesn't want to tell me. I don't care.

"My father was an engineer, born in Rotterdam, and my mother a refugee who was born in Vienna, Austria. I was born in Aalten, province of Gelderland, and went to school there. My older brother serves with the Dutch Navy in the Dutch East Indies. My parents are dead. I haven't seen my brother since the beginning of the war ..." and on and on like that, a whole page long. It was an exercise for a writer; I enjoyed doing this. I handed it to the personnel manager in his office and made sure I saw where he put it. On purpose I had typed the "life story" on a piece of yellow paper to find it more easily when I looked for it. I didn't plan to leave it with him too long. I loathed the idea of giving so much written information on myself. But there had been no choice. The price for entry into Kolberg's employ was a supply of information on myself. After all, it's a Ministry, an official body; I would have made myself suspicious to refuse it. Four days later, when I knew the personnel manager was out of town, I went into his office with an arm full of wood, took the yellow paper, and put it in my pocket. If he would look for it, I would pretend that I had never given it to him and write him another one. Maybe a stupid and feeble lie, but the idea of information on me being sent to Berlin didn't let me sleep.

It was Christmas and we had a big office party in the Schwan. With plenty of good food and wine and schnapps. Everyone a bit drunk, a typical German after-dinner game started, a game called *double entendre*. In fact it has no name. It is a conversation in veiled sexual terminology. It goes like this:

HE: Would you like another little schnapps?
SHE: Is that all you have to offer?
HE: The rest of the bottle is still under the cork.
SHE: (laughs) Don't let it run out.
HE: I wouldn't mind, beautiful lady.

SHE: Do you think I can take it?

HE: Better to try than to study the project.

SHE: My husband looks at us all the time.

HE: Don't worry, he seems to be occupied with Mrs. Pohl.

I liked this kind of flirtation; it seemed so much easier than picking up a girl at a dance hall.

I tried taking Stella up to my room, but didn't get too far. Kolberg and Fräulein Blom kept an eye on me. One of the first things Kolberg had told me, "I don't want you to have any affairs with any women in this office or in this town. I don't want you to make friends with anyone outside this office, either. If I find out that you do, you are fired."

He obviously had his reasons for keeping me in isolation from the rest of the world; I just wish he would have sanctioned my interest in Stella.

Gone was the freedom of the roaming sailor, I was now an official in a Ministry and had to behave differently. I hated that more than anything. Between Christmas and New Year I moved from the Schwan; the propreitor complained about having to open the door for me after ten (God knows where I managed to hang out so late). I got a room in another house, at the very top of the building, my own key, without having to pass through anyone's flat, and the main door open all night.

I made a date for New Year's Eve with a girl I had met at the Christmas party. We left together shortly after midnight of the New Year (New Year's Eve, next to Carnival, is the time when anything is permitted in Germany), and I took her up to my room. It was on her way home. In bed I celebrated my cure from the Knight's illness, my new employ with Kolberg, and the New Year, 1945, which would be the end of the war. Gertrude confided in me, because a foreigner is politically trustworthy, that her father is a lawyer, in jail somewhere for opposing the Nazis, and that she herself hates the *Sheisshitler* and the entire *Scheisse*. This kind of girl I had not met before in Germany. She was articulate, outspoken, fearless, and mad at the Nazis. Thus 1945 started all right. As I walked her home through snow-covered fields, in a cold starlit night, with not a sound in the universe, she shouted drunkenly: "Scheisshitler, Scheissadolf, go to hell."

I had to calm her down, and she was cross with me that I

didn't help her scream curses in the wind. I had another few months to go, and a Jew arrested and a German girl arrested would not be the same kind of thing. Just a few more months and maybe only weeks; they were fighting in East Prussia, in Czechoslovakia, in the Ardennes. Hitler had had it.

In the beginning of January they gave me a letter addressed to *"Alle Dienststellen der Polizei und der SS im Reich"* (to all offices of the police and the SS in the Reich) to allow Jan Gerrit Overbeek free passage and extend to him all possible aid on his trips on behalf of the *Luftfahrtministerium*. This letter was enough to buy myself a ticket (first class) and report to Mr. Kolberg in the Pension Friedrichsbahnhof in Berlin. Trains between main cities ran quite regularly. Occasional stops while battalions of POW's repaired the railway, but ultimately one got there. In the big town, swarming with people, German, foreign, I felt really well and safe for the first time since I had crossed the border in November '43. In Berlin, with a letter like the one I had in my pocket, I could also wander around and not easily be checked by Kolberg. I found bars and coffeehouses on the Kurfürstendamm and around the Alexanderplatz, with music, alcohol, cigarettes on the black market (a packet of Ernte was 80 marks), and girls. I liked Berlin. My job was hardly strenuous. I had to take some letters to certain officials in the Air Ministry on Friedrichstrasse. I delivered my letters in large brown envelopes, turned about, and said good-bye.

"'Heil Hitler,' we say here," a sergeant snarled at me.

"Good-bye," I said.

"Heil Hitler," said the man. He raised his arm.

I raised mine but said nothing. No sergeant in an Air Ministry can have you shot for not saying "Heil Hitler" if you are a foreigner. "I am a Dutchman," I said, to explain the reason for my refusal to greet with the *deutsche Gruss*.

"Out," he said. I closed the door quietly.

At other times my letters went to other people in the building. People who didn't care whether I said "Heil Hitler" or "Good morning." But what was in the envelopes I didn't know, nor was I particularly interested to break one open and find out. It all seemed safer than sitting on the deck of the *Matthias Stinnes 18*. And safer than in hospitals without a disease. As a student of history, Berlin was the right place for me. In the lobby of the Pension Friedrichsbahnhof usually a colourful bunch of people crowded for dinner. Among the many highranking officers, I saw a man with red stripes along his trousers. General Vlassov, the porter said. They spoke Russian and German at the tops of their voices and a little orchestra played the latest hits.

My room was not very big, but comfortable. Kolberg had an office in the same Friedrichstrasse on the third floor of an innocuous building. I came home whenever I liked, never expecting his calls before 10 A.M. But somhow (by asking the porter, of course) he found out that I came home late, two or three in the morning. He asked me up to his office. He and Fräulein Blom were bundling papers in a dark, half-empty office.

"Overbeek," he said, "I am sorry, but I have to discharge you. Against my instruction not to fraternize with the rest of the population, you come and go and do what you like. You spend your evenings in the company of all sorts of people. " Did he know about the little Latvian girl called Sonya?

"I am sorry, Mr. Kolberg. I am very sorry, but I can't sit in my room all day, I have no one to talk to."

"But I have warned you before, it's the condition you accepted when I employed you."

I felt ashamed for my childish behaviour. Of course, he was right. I had promised not to talk to anyone, I should keep my word. He must have sensed that I was genuinely sorry. "I will forgive you for the very last time. Why don't you go to your room and read a bit of Nietzsche?"

The reason I couldn't go on reading Nietzsche all day and night was that Nietzsche had done something to my mind no other book had ever done to me. It turned me into an *bermensch*, a fellow without heart or soul. Nothing but cold-blooded logical calculation, nothing but inhuman distance from other humans. The *bermensch* looks at the world and the people and snarls and laughs from his Olympic heights. *"Die Welt ist nicht als ein Abklatsch weicher Gefühle* (the world is nothing but an impression of weak feelings)" or something of this sort. At the height of my Olympic mountain among generals and high officials of a doomed Empire, I searched for a trace of soft feelings. Any sort of humanity was better than none. I had hated to share the humanity of Jews when they were asked to die for it, but I felt warmth and kindness towards miserable-looking foreigners and poor working-class Germans. Berlin had another face. Not everything was dressed in swastikas. Among the workers in the Wedding district, among the small people on the railway stations, among the ordinary *Landsers* who cared nothing for Hitler and nothing for the war, I found a glimmer in the eyes I hadn't seen since Seitz, our Red burgomaster, left the Goethehof. I saw the universal sufferance of the small man, victim of Fascist dictatorship and Capitalist exploitation. The soldiers of the Red Army pushing through Silesia and East Prussia to Berlin were my heroes. I loved them, if anything, even more than the air forces of the British and the Americans.

From Berlin we travelled by car to Hamburg. Kolberg drove an Opel Kapitän, and I sat next to him providing the conversation. We talked about everything that came to my mind. But what usually came to my mind was some garbled kind of philosophy, a mixture of Nietzsche's *"Ewige Wiederkehr"* and Marxian supposition that all men are equal. I didn't trust him and I didn't distrust him. I just couldn't care less whether he was going to deliver me to the Gestapo or not. I was convinced he wouldn't, or he would have done so before. I knew he needed me, but I couldn't figure out why. In Hamburg we stayed in the pompous Hotel Die Vier Jahreszeiten overlooking the Alster. The Alster was frozen, and the town looked shabby and half bombed-out.

There was nowhere to go in Hamburg, and Kolberg was too nearby. I usually spent the days reading on my bed in the luxury suite and the nights amongst diamond-studded, fur-clad wives of officers and rich industrialists in the air raid shelter of the hotel. The proximity of wealth increased my hatred against the wealthy. No longer did I hate only the Nazis in uniform, I also loathed the rich who benefited most by this government. When the war is over there will be a revolution, I dreamed, Germany will rise again as a fortress of the Capitalists and the Fascists. Nazism is the whip of the rich against the poor; of the strong against the weak. I myself might be a *bermensch*, a Stalin. Brute force and power to smash the Nazi dragon, nothing else, nothing less will do. From Hamburg I went back to Dillenburg, from Dillenburg to Berlin, and forwards and backwards. I was usually on the railway. It was better to be nowhere than anywhere in particular.

Hamburg, 4 march 1945. Sunday evening, 9:40 P.M. (a touch of Prussian historian).

One should write if one has something to say, I once read. To "something" I always added the word "new." That's why I can write nothing longer than a long letter. The more I read, the more I know, the more I am convinced that there is nothing new to be said. To write what has been known before I call plagiarism. To write things I don't know I can't do either. It might have been said before. Rather live with the melancholy of one who cannot write, than live with the apparent satisfaction of the creative (person). I couldn't stand the ridicule.

In spite of all this, I make plans and notes for bigger work, convinced that I will carry them out gradually, it's only to correct my style while writing. Besides writing requires discipline of thought, and thoughts will have to be expressed logically. Writing means creating order in a chaos of sensibilities, feelings, thoughts. It requires courage to *want* to create order and strength, to make it. But first of all, one has to want something, and suddenly I know, I will and I shall. It will be a wrestling match against my other "self." But he who *wants* is stronger; one day I will win. Is that a way to start a letter? Well, my letters to you start like that. Stop. Another question: What shall I write to her? That I love her, that I am isolated, that I dream of our meeting again soon? Write her that I am well and hope that she is all right? It's hard to repeat forever what I feel at all times. It would be easy *to say* something, not just talk etc., etc ... I have seen a lot, maybe too much. It has to be like that. It's my fate to taste the bitterness of an inner split, again, and again, and again. I am young and old, naïve and sophisticated, energetic and phlegmatic at the same time. All this in turn or at the same time. I am both sensitive and rough, I love the South and the North, everything southern is my true nature. If you can't love yourself it's sad. The South is slow and mystical, secretive, unclear, promising, lazy. The North is clear, of simple beauty, a rough splendour, militant, stubborn, cruel against all that is weak. The question is like this (a note for later): Nietzsche has seduced me with his teachings. Torn me away from everything Christian and moral, from everything dubious. I don't believe any longer that man is good *in spite* of everything, I don't believe in democracy, not even in the worker, in the world of machines and collectives. It's all finished. Maybe he gave me back to myself? How else would his words have found an echo in my desert?

All rights to the individual, freedom and justice to the special one, quality not quantity. I already start to wonder whether everyone has a right to live. It's not easy to grasp these new ideas, to sort out the pros and cons for someone like me, child of Humanism and Communism. The time has come, I must cross the bridge into a real world, a cold and lonely world, coming from a world that protected me with soft lights of dusk and sounds of Mozart. What is the goal? To define a goal and live for it? I interpret Nietzsche and his world: as a world of high intelligence, laughing seriousness, a world of the strong and courageous. I read Nietzsche and with me is the sentence:"He who has the power, also has the right." And I know who will have the power. The physically superior, the beautiful, the splendid man. Power over whom? Power over the mentally inferior. If I realize that to be true, all that is human in me is desperate. I see a clear danger ahead, the danger of a perversion: If the world is only a place for the physically superior and the mental aristocracy, and the people have the spirit, and only the mind of the people is down to earth, terrestrial even in its myth and symbols, then a ruling class that has left the spirit of the people "are wheels that roll out of their own."

I have an idea of truth about this world. I can see the power of a future ruler, but is the lowest worth to be ruled by the highest? It doesn't become the clever to win over the stupid. First a mass has to be created worth being ruled over, or does one wish to celebrate cheap victories? Now that I get tired, the Orient rises, soothing hands and sweet melodies ... Night has begun. Strange. I never felt lonely at night. Is dusk not warmer than the light of the sun? They say in the evenings the fog rises and it's cold, I can't understand this. Nothing is colder to the eyes and the heart than sunlight shining on people and things ... and yet nothing more dangerous than the night. At night children can get lost because they cannot see, they only sense and follow smells and the lights of the fireflies. Measuring the depth of this world, I got tired ... The great Man must be able to lead two lives ...

These are the kinds of things I wrote. It reveals only one thing now: deep depression, probably sparked off by the imminent end of the war.

They didn't hang them and they didn't shoot them, they wouldn't have known whom to start with. In Kellinghusen the Nazis disappeared with the swastikas, and people just didn't greet with "Heil Hitler" when they entered a shop. It would have been in "bad taste". Hitler was dead, Dönitz had capitulated, the last remnants of the army were taken prisoner or choked the roads as tired, hungry men, walking back from Denmark. They might give them a drink or a piece of bread. But on the whole the civilians didn't have too much of it themselves to give away. Peace had broken out. Again everyone was for himself and God for all of us.

I told Kolberg after we had the news of Hitler's suicide that I was a Jew from Vienna and not Jan Overbeek. He took it as a Prussian officer. Without moving a muscle. But he did say, "Oh." And in this one "Oh" coming from him was everything I had wanted to hear for two years. "Oh" meant: So you are smarter than I thought. Marvellous. Congratulations. You won.

"Fräulein Blom is half-Jewish, Overbeek." It was my turn to say "Oh", and as he was obviously a nice man, because I was still alive thanks to the job he gave me in the Ministry, I said, "Oh", but it was a polite "Oh." I didn't really care whether she was half-Jewish. Half-Jews had not been in the same boat. Some half-Jews even served in the German Army and some in the *Arbeitsdienst*. It's too complicated to explain who was considered half-Jewish and eligible to live as a second-class citizen. I never found out exactly how it worked. Some half-Jews were allowed to serve the fatherland and others sent to concentration camps. So Fräulein Blom is half-Jewish, so what? He didn't impress me and looked for something else.

"I have done valuable work for the Allies," he said, and I could only vaguely guess the exact meaning of this. How had he done valuable work? By searching the metals of Messerschmitts for faults? By building the German cyclotron in a disguised factory near Kellinghusen? I saw it once. It looked like a big machine, standing ten or fifteen feet from the ground, and grey like the undercoating on a flying saucer. I didn't dare to ask: What exactly do you mean? In fact, I didn't want to know. No answer he gave me would have been the correct one. As I must have looked skeptical at his revelation, he added, "Listen, Overbeek, stay here until the British are here, and they must be here today or tomorrow, and you will see. You have helped me to help them. They will appreciate it."

"Or you will appreciate it?" I thought. What am I supposed to be, your private Jew? I didn't say this, after all, he had helped me, not knowing that I was a Jew, but I was alive and well all the same. It probably was my turn to do him a good turn. It was probably on me now, to show generosity. And if he hadn't expected it, I might have been enthusiastic to help him. But he did expect me to act as some sort of cover up, why else would he need me around? He might have helped the Allies while he helped the Germans and himself as well. The cyclotron construction had certainly kept him from the front and out of uniform. What more could an able-bodied German ask for? The cyclotron had kept him and the scientific staff, of whom I remember only a Dr. Wideroe, a Norwegian, in their slippers far away from the battles of Stalingrad and Voronezh. What the Army looked like I could just see by walking down to the main road; why should I stay and by staying cover a man who must obviously have something coming that might be unpleasant, or why else would he need my cover? No, I didn't feel generous. I did not see why I should hang around a day longer than necessary in this shitty country.

"No, Mr. Kolberg," I said, "I'm afraid I am not interested in staying, I want to go back to Amsterdam to see how my family is doing."

"You are eighteen now, Mr. Overbeek. You have no trade and no profession. I think it could be arranged that you get a scholarship to study in England or the United States. Don't you want to study languages and philosophy?"

113

"I want to study a lot of things, but for the time being I want to go back home."

"Don't be so impatient, Mr. Overbeek."

"But I am."

"You can't go yet anyway, not until the Allies are here."

"All right. I will wait a few days."

The next days I spent copying blueprints and letters, sheets of instructions and more blueprints. God knows why and for whom. We took the papers out of one grey box and put them back into another. The boxes were stored away somewhere in the back of the barn. I went around smiling. Talking openly to Jan, the Czech driver of our lorry, about getting out of this place. He was thinking of taking the lorry back to Prague where he could sell it or start a business with it. Everyone I knew in the village, Italian POW's, Russians and Ukrainians, Dutch and French labourers, they all were in some sort of business. One bought, or rather, requisitioned a hundred hams, the other had found a stock of butter. One came with the keys to a store that was abandoned, the other knew how to get hold of a good BMW motorcycle. Why didn't I steal a car or butter or a ton of lard? Because I didn't care. I didn't need it. What shall I do with it? Walk a hundred miles with a weight of butter on my head and sell it to a baker? Jan the Czech helped some Ukrainians to empty an Army depot and brought me a pair of high brown boots. I liked brown, and the boots would be useful for the long walk back to Amsterdam. It didn't look like there would be transport too soon.

I saw the British tanks entering Kellinghusen. The Second Army handed out Player's and sweets, not to everyone. Just to the girls and children. The townspeople were either passive or helped to show the Tommies the way. The beer houses were full and where there were souvenirs for sale, business flourished. Coming back from a stroll in town just to stare at the Tommies, who said hello when you stared long enough at them, I found a whole regiment of troops in the grounds of our farm. There was a note somewhere that said, "Second Army. T-Force. Keep Out." But because I lived there, even if it took me a few minutes to persuade the guard that I did, I was allowed to pass.

I had also gone to town this morning to enquire about transport down south and so on to Holland. The Dutch boys in the cafés didn't quite know where I came from. I looked better dressed than they did, had this cultural air of the "different" person. Who the hell was I? What did I want from them? How could I explain to them that I was just one of them, while I knew that I wasn't? Two lorries full of foreigners had already left for the next stop south, the camp at Lüneburg. Someone promised me I could get on the next lorry after that, but naturally no one was too helpful to a complete outsider. I don't think they thought I was an enemy, but they didn't quite know what to think. Who was I? Who am I? A Jew? A Dutchman? A Nazi? An Austrian? How did I get here all by myself into this ugly hole without working for a farmer, without having to be in a labour camp? Must be someone special. They didn't trust it and moved away from me.

Kolberg tried a last time to persuade me to stay. I said definitely no, at least not for the time being. I've first to go back and see whether my sister and girl friend are still alive; after a few weeks I could always come back here. With pedantic Prussian red tape I got a letter that gave me leave of absence "for the time being," but no discharge from the Air Ministry, which did or did no longer exist.

The war is over. Everyone says "hurrah", I say "hurrah" and feel sick. Too much and too quickly eaten from a tin of corned beef someone on the road had thrown into our lorry. After the corned beef without bread, I had also gobbled up a tin of greasy sweet bacon. nothing to drink with it. And while everybody says, "Where are you going? I am going home," I was even too sick to talk. I just leant against a tree in the grounds of the Lüneburg transit camp and tried not to vomit. Besides the vomiting, the diarrhoea. Life is flowing out of me, I am dissolving. I don't think I will survive the peace. The war is barely two weeks over and I am afraid of all sorts of illnesses. A district nurse from Birmingham thinks I might have typhoid or malaria or cholera or something terrible and should be lying down in their hospital. The hospital is a disused tower in the round, and there are beds everywhere, not just in neat rows, but beds like in an emergency hospital behind the front.

Seeing the skeletons from Belsen (Bergen-Belsen is only a few kilometres from where we are) who stare at me from behind a world I have never seen, seeing open flesh wounds of people who had somehow survived as German guinea pigs,

115

talking to a girl who had lost her parents, brothers, sisters, and half her mind on a march for three weeks from Buchenwald, walking at gunpoint for a hundred miles and those who fell were shot in the neck by a Ukrainian SS guard, seeing the tears of crazy toothless old men of twenty-five, and gay children with one finger poking up their nose and one eye missing, playing with toys with one crippled hand, probably broken by some alcoholic cab driver in an SS uniform, I seem to have neither cholera nor diphtheria, no typhoid and no consumtion. I am just sick, to death, and believe it's the corned beef and greasy bacon eaten without bread. I am not well and I have a problem with identity. I know who I am, that's not the problem; I just don't wish to be who I am. It's useless to be Jan Overbeek (who knows, maybe they will think I am a collaborator; after all, I lived in the Vier Jahreszeiten in Hamburg and not in Bergen-Belsen all those last weeks). But even if no one thinks that (and I could do nothing if anyone did), I still have no use for Jan Overbeek. Nor have I use for J.L.

J.L. is by nationality Austrian but probably stateless by now. All human refuse found after the war, all those wrecks who popped up from nowhere, are again redivided into nationalities and shipped home. I have no home and no nationality. There is no one left in Vienna and I can't live again in Amsterdam. Jaap Granaat, even if alive, will no longer be paid by the Refugee Committee to take me into his home; I have only one chance to be welcomed and that would be in Palestine, where my parents arrived from Vienna. I knew this from a Red Cross letter I had received via London in '41. Palestine is the only place I want to go right now, with a short detour via Amsterdam to see whether Ditta, my little sister, and her foster parents are still alive. I am not in that much of a hurry because I have no chance to get permission to enter Palestine. Only 1,500 people per month are allowed in. Why should I be one of them?

We all had to register in front of a long table to get some sort of identity — the people from Belsen don't even have a false one — and as all nationalities and races queue in front of me, from Chinese to Algerian, I translate my name into what I think is Hebrew and say, "My name is Jakov Chaklan, born on the 10th of February 1927 in Haifa, which makes me Palestinian."

"Well, how do you do?" says a young soldier in an ironic Oxford accent, and hands me a new piece of paper which I put next to my passport and my letters from Kolberg.

"I want to go to Holland," I said. "That's where the Germans picked me up. As a Palestinian they might have interned me, as a Jew the risk was too big; that's why I went to work in Germany." There are too many behind me in the line waiting for identification. Who cares who and what I am anyway? And as Jakov Chaklan, Palestinian, they fly me in an old Dakota transporter to Brussels. The first time in the air, with a load of ex-Lüneburg cases (the worst they kept behind, not to upset the Belgians), I feel like in the Prater again — gliding through the air. It's a laugh and a scream. And everybody in the plane has the greatest time of his life. (Had those Dakotas flown us out a few years earlier, we might have been less hysterical with pleasure.) A plane full of happy faces and one has constantly to be reminded by a young soldier that someone is dying in the back underneath a blanket.

In Brussels there is a bed for everyone from the plane, in a school. I was used to better accommodation lately, and didn't much like the two Tunisians next to me, who talked and probably fucked all night. I decided Brussels wasn't the place to wait for transport to Amsterdam which might or might never arrive. On all corners of the town American soldiers play music, march up and down, salute, and hand flags over. The children are happy, jumping up and down. German soldiers, too, used to make music, march up and down and hand flags from one to another, but they didn't share out sweets and cigarettes. And this is ultimately the difference between the armies. The music alone won't do. Easy to hitchhike to the Dutch border. One just had to look like a prodigal son. The confusion at the border guarded by English and Dutch troops is great. A Palestinian resident of the Netherlands back from Germany? Well, why not? There are also Mongolian Russians, Danish Eskimos, Indians and Kuwaitis from Abyssinia passing through. All that are left after the Third Reich caved in (not enough cement, Mr. Streicher; not enough iron in the bones, Mr. Keitel) scrambles back to what they believe is home.

The first town in liberated Holland is badly lit by Philips lamps. Philips has always been Eindhoven for me. A town, it

117

seemed, created for people who wish to work in electronics. In May '45 plenty of schools spread straw in classrooms to sleep transit passengers. I seem to have returned to the *Matthias Stinnes* — the suite in Hamburg never existed. I have nothing and can't leave it anywhere. I have a bundle of clothes in a sailor's kit bag, but no place to stall it. The treasure in the bag consists of the diaries, the letters to my sweetheart with the firm breasts. "My darling," it says there in red ink, "I love you more than anything in the world; because of you I will have to survive this war." And I wasn't ironical when I wrote it. Cilly Levitus is her name and I have to find her. Orpheus back from the underworld looking for his Eurydice. *Ach, ich habe dich verloren, meine Ruh'ist nun dahin, o, wär ich nie geboren, weh dass ich auf Erden bin.* (I have lost you. My peace is gone, I wish I had never been born, O, how I suffer this world.) Ach and *O* and *Weh*. The vocabulary of the unhappy romantic lover in Gluck's Germanic version of Orpheus who actually mourns the loss of his youth.

I am just an ordinary romantic hero in a bad play. I love as soon as I hear myself pronounce the words "I love you." If I say, "Your eyes, your lips are mine, I think of you and only of you," I do not only repeat the words of a popular hit word for word, I really mean it. It might have been the Viennese education or the Dutch education or the German experience, but sentiments were (and still are) expressed in phrases, maybe to prevent us from a silence that may allow for second thoughts. One way or another, at eighteen I was so full of words like love, beauty, marvel, eternity, forever, that I could probably have drifted above Eindhoven, instead of walking through it, by the very sound their gas produces, leaking from my head.

I took the treasure with me, bundled in a brown piece of wrapping paper, and left the bag in the school. Let them walk away with my last pair of socks; I carried my "essential existence" with me in a packet. My "essential existence," as I like to call it with Nietzschean paraphrase, is my writing. Whatever is black or red on white cannot be removed. The spoken word is a prayer, the written word a sacrifice. Every written word is sacrosanct, it can never be thrown away. Not if I wrote it. Now I have cupboards and baskets full of holy scriptures, then in '45 I had only this one bundle of papers, and maybe some more papers that might have survived with my sister in Amsterdam.

118

A priest in search of his congregation, I ask everyone in sight whether they have heard of a girl called C. L. And someone has. C. L.? Originally from Frankfurt? Yes. A nurse? Yes. Brown hair? Yes. Blue eyes? About nineteen or twenty? Yes. It's her. It must be her, working as a nurse in one of the hospitals. I put my best shirt on and carry my own weight in paper to the other end of town. Is there a nurse called C. L. working in your hospital?

"Shall we call her for you? Please wait downstairs in the hall." I am even too nervous to smoke. I pretend serenity. Stoic indifference. Someone hollers down the stairs, beaming all over the face. In the same uniform I had seen her in last time, when she still looked after the babies in the crèche.

And I thought you were dead, she smiled.

Thought I was dead? Thought *I* was dead? Lived through eighty air raids and she thought I was dead? Of course I am dead, of course I am dead. Yes, I am dead, I said, and that's for you. I handed her the parcel.

What shall I do with it now? I am in the middle of work. What's in it?

Papers, I say faintly, letters for you.

Let's meet after work, and then you will give them to me.

I didn't want to take them with me. It would have been better to burn them right on the spot in the hall. "They are yours."

She took them, not very amused, having to look after a parcel for the rest of the day.

Not quite convinced that I was awake, alive and not a ghost, I needed another confrontation. I didn't give up yet.

All right, let's meet tonight.

Come to think of it, she said, I can't. I might as well tell you, someone will collect me.

You have a boy friend?

An English soldier. Very sweet boy.

A boy friend? An English soldier?

What's wrong with that?

Nothing. So we shan't meet.

Yes, we must meet. We must talk. How about this Saturday afternoon where I live with my little sister Jutta; remember her? You won't recognize her. She has grown. Remember she was a child?

The war was over and language had lost its meaning.

Words of love, words of faith and belief, words of hope and eternal devotion, words of kisses and clouds. All useless. C. L. cured me from eighteen years' accumulated Austrian-Jewish schmaltz. It froze in the ice of her healthy, normal laugh over so much madness. As I obviously couldn't share her bed together with an English soldier (though she could have asked me, the bitch! I hadn't even been allowed to touch her cunt with my finger!), I left. Still a little weak after this heavy operation in which I had been amputated of romantic love by a children's nurse, I went back to my straw on the floorboards of the school's chemistry laboratory to sleep it over. I certainly should not have been alive anyway. Of course, it wasn't my fault that I was still among the living, yet it was. I had received my punishment for being lucky and intelligent. By surviving I had made a very grave mistane, and what looked like success to others was for me proof that I had failed miserably. Why should C. have expected me to be alive, just because I had lacked the fantasy to imagine anything else?

School for Alchemy

As a child of ten I had wanted to be Prince Mishkin, and it took me a few months to discover that this is impossible. Less than ten years later I decided *to become* a writer, and it took me fifteen years to learn that it is impossible *to become* anything but a postman, a man who sells his spare time for a regular salary. In 1945 existence and identity were still a dubious affair. Too many proofs were required, too much evidence had to be produced. I couldn't accept the simple fact that I was still alive. I might have lost a girl friend to another man, but at the same time I had won the war against Hitler and Goebbels, by outliving them. And I had also outlived quite a number of lesser supermen who would gladly have skinned me alive in a concentration camp medical experiment, f.i., to observe in the name of science if a man can survive cancer cells injected into his liver. I had won the war after a bit of trouble, a kind of fistfight in a saloon; checking my belongings I noticed I had nothing left but my bare skin. Everything else had gone. No Zionism, no idealism. No love and no hatred and no language. Worst of all — no language.

When I was two, our maid Mitzi left and went back to her village on the Czech border of Lower Austria. She had come from Hadres to Vienna because her brothers were in the habit of beating her up when drunk. She went back because we probably couldn't afford her after Wall Street or whatever that means collapsed, burying most Viennese businessmen under its debris. Or maybe we could have afforded her, but my parents were afraid she might once more fall asleep with their male offspring in her arms, letting a pot with boiling laundry put out the flames on the gas stove. I still choke easily with fear, emotion, overfatigue, and when in the arms of large women.

Whatever the reason, Mitzi was gone. She had taught me to

121

call things by their name, a *Reindl*, a *Schweindl*, a *Heferl*, a *Tepp* (a pot, a pig, a cup, a stupid ass — in Viennese jargon). Without her I didn't know what to say. Proceeded to look for words, could never get enough of them, ran around looking for Mitzi's breasts to feed and her lap to ride on.

> *hoppa, hoppa reita*
> *wenn er fällt da schreit a*
> *fällt a in den grabn*
> *fressn ihn die rabn*
> *fällt a in den sumpf*
> *mocht da reita — plumps*

Feet whip up and down, up and down, suddenly knees are spread and — plop — a child falls to the ground. She let me ride her knees, warmed her naked body with me in her iron bedstead in the kitchen, and taught me by the way a few simple words. (Isn't that what literature is ultimately all about?) Mitzi was love. My mother had two other children to attend to as well. I had it from both women, the milk of literature, from my Jewish moral, respectable mother, and from generations of tough and half-mad Austrian peasants. I needed them both. (I might still need them) *hoppa, hoppa reita* — and Mitzi had vanished like a horse.

> *vom himmel fall ich zuar eard*
> *un kauf mia ein grosses pfeard*
> *dann reit ich schnäll davon*
> *und kreig an luftballon.*

Poetry is the sublimation of all that's good in life, fantasy the asylum of its malcontent. In German my wish-dream rhymed. I made it rhyme with Mitzi's departure. I would have been after her on the horse I would buy one day, to chase her breasts to the ends of the world.

Everything depended on words back in 1929, on right words to be spoken rightly, but any good words will do. People can take them home and search them for deeper meanings; out of their pockets where they have tucked away the words, they produce coins and hand them to the poet, kiss him on both cheeks, and stroke his blond curls. The poet might have talked to himself, about something that is on his mind, there always will be aunts and uncles around who claim there was a message in it addressed to them personally.

Language was my real problem again and, this time, to find my own nourishment in myself. I needed language to lift what had dropped into the Danube and Rhine and a few other mainstreams of confusion and misery. I needed a language and the time to find it before I could carry on. I knew an antiquated Austrian, a fluent bargeman's Dutch, and a few sentences in every other European language, enough to ask for a glass of water. I had been a writer all my life, since Mitzi left and again after I left Hartl's school.

In '45 I had difficulties in ecpressing even the simplest sentence. I couldn't make plausible what I had to tell. I could talk about the years in Germany but no one could understand. I needed the understanding of an entire world from which I had seceded on 20 June 1943. Cilly L. had finished my love, my friend Fritz Sofer was nowhere. The ears that could listen had moved into the eastern Mediterranean. My little sister and Louis and Alice Polak had returned from the underworld, but my friends had gone.

With Ida, my new girl friend, I could share a straw mattress. But love is language, a common language — I thought then. To talk, to find words again, I had to go south to what I expected to be home. Ida travelled with me south to the border. Even without moving her breasts and behind she could stop cars, military and civilian, at eighty miles an hour. All my arm-waving was ridiculous gymnastics compared to her right leg slightly set forward. An unavoidable attachment to the dirty movies in their minds, the drivers had to put up with me.

I was the Eskimo with a wife to swap against a dogsledge ride to other hunting grounds. A wife, a faithful wife, I learned on this ride, means property. Love and devotion are properties and means to acquire definite material advantages. Of course one must "love" one's wife. A wife of one's own has value for private use or barter. I was not really leaving Holland for Palestine. I left a playground of teen-age romantic ideas for a land of mature manhood. Cynical exploitation of a female is the birthright of the male, accepted by both parties as the way of things, but made obscure by the insane notion of "happy couple together," a state of human disgrace also

123

known as "marriage," a kind of contract between master and slave that allows for a certain amount of interchange of roles.

Seven years of National-Socialist homosexual rule of the stronger over the weaker and I had turned cynical without so much as trying to emulate the Nazism in the air. Inhaling and exhaling the foul breath of its dark and brutal homosexuality had apparently been enough, and preferable to the inhaling of cyanide in bolted strong rooms. I still can recall the taste of her tongue that must have tasted the lie on mine, when I kissed her good-bye, told her I loved her and hoped she would soon be joining me. In sight of a painted tree trunk manned by soldiers across a country lane we smiled a "so long" and "see you soon." The jump across this hurdle I had to make all by myself. To keep moving ahead into something unknown was, strictly speaking, a private affair.

It hadn't beeen difficult to pass the Belgian border in '43 on the voyage of the *Matthias Stinnes*, the Germans had trusted me to be Jan Overbeek, why should the Allies question my new papers? I was Jakov Chaklan, Palestinian, without difficulty until I reach the French border at Maubeuge. As I stepped off the train, I was arrested and marched off by a French Army corporal together with two Poles I had never seen before in my life. *Un-deux, Un-deux*, first I smiled, thought it was a joke. Whoever would get it in his mad mind to arrest me? Even the Gestapo had never done anything as outrageous as that. When it was hinted that I am suspected of big a German soldier who had escaped from a POW camp, or an SS man who is trying to make it to Spain, I became furious. I might not have been Jakov Chaklan the Palestinian, but I certainly was a Jew back from Germany. I couldn't explain that in French and no one wished to listen. I was a "suspect" and I wasn't really surprised. As I didn't trust myself, why should others trust me?

I was pushed through a door marked "Intelligence" and had to lower my trousers. The man from MI-6 must have had considerable experience with cocks. He could tell right away what no German Nazi doctor ever discovered. This man has a little bit of his foreskin missing, ergo this man is a Jew. Established now beyond doubt of Allied intelligence that I am Jewish, I asked for a ticket to Haifa and got a travel voucher and food coupons until Marseilles. In Marseilles I would be handed the second half of my ticket, I was told, expecting that the intelligence officer in Marseilles would make me recite the entire Bible in Hebrew.

A reception committee of middle-aged ladies received me on the Gare du Nord. I was the first Palestinian passing through, and was pointed out to Jewish refugees who promptly asked me if I could help them to get a "Certificate." Everyone wanted to go to Palestine for some reason, even those who didn't look in the least bit like a Pioneer. Everyone wanted to leave Paris. Paris (Arc de Triomphe, Champs Elysées, Jean Gabin, Emile Zola, Dreyfus trial, and hot chestnuts stands) was hot and overcast, full of shabbily dressed people and dossed-up soldiers. I had to change stations and spent the day with a girl I met by chance on the Gare du Nord. A strange coincidental meeting, as I had boarded a train with the same girl in Vienna in 1938 and we had been together in a refugee camp in The Hague. I remember her as robust, tall, fair-headed, and Germanic-looking. She was called Metta Lande and worked for an organization, something to do with illegal transports to break the blockade of British warships along the coast of Palestine. Why she did it? Because it's important work. Why not go to Palestine herself and help build the country? Because she was helping the country by being in Paris. For an hour or so I thought of staying in Paris as well, if a girl could work in an illegal organization, I, with all my experience as an undercover superagent, should certainly do the same.

"I feel I should stay here, Metta, and help you. But I am a coward. I couldn't help anyone. I have lost something. I have lost everything in fact. My purpose in life, my idealism, my language, my family."

"What awaits you in Palestine?"

"Parents. First things first. I must meet my parents."

"That's something else."

I didn't believe in my excuse, though she did maybe. I simply didn't care for others who had reemerged from their dugouts. I just couldn't care less. I had dug my own shelter when they went by charter to Auschwitz. I hated them both again — Jews and Germans. The first because they aroused my pity, the second because they could (I thought) claim my gratitude. I had survived as one of them. An Aryan non-Aryan, which made me a silent accomplice in a massacre. I hated myself and them, doubly. Once for my soft self-pity and once for my smug self-pride. Let the Jews go to America, India, Brazil, or to hell. But of course I didn't say that to Metta. I said, "First things first." The truth I wouldn't have admitted, certainly not to myself. The truth was that any additional excitement was superfluous. Normal breathing was already too fast, left me breathless most of the nights. Or to put it differently: To the dead state of my mind even the slightest vibration beyond ordinary breathing was too much.

Courage had left me. Cowardice numbed my senses. I was ashamed and sick with myself. My face was an immobile mask revealing not the slightest damage, just like the façade of this town that had not been damaged in air raids. What kind of human being am I, scared to death by the squeak of car tyres, moved to tears by seeing others cry?

"I am useless, Metta, I am a corpse. All I want is to go home and sleep. I can't stand on my legs." I had a *couchette* to Marseilles and a dram of sunshine and happy faces crying. I hadn't lost everything yet, apparently, I still thought I had to be sentimental. "Let's be sentimental, time goes so quick." I am the generation of the tango, a child of courteous pleasant-ries, noble feelings, simple phrases. Half gentleman-crimi-nal, half Pioneer-con man. Travelling as usual with a false-identity under my pillow. The British Consul in Marseilles handled my special case with the respect due to a Lüneburg Transit Camp Identity Card. "Jakov Chaklan, born 10.2.27 in Haifa, Palestinian? Maybe and maybe not?" A philosophi-cal decision of my life expressed in H. M. Government terms. What the Consul in fact said, was: His Majesty's Government has no objection if I would go on calling myself Chaklan, Smith, or Brown for the rest of my life, but a birth certificate issued by the Mandate Government might prove my claim. The Consul was the first intelligent man who challenged my identity — I thought the entire British race is brilliant (in spite of my experience in Lüneburg and Maubeuge).

Instead of loathing their guts, which I should have, because they barred the entry of Jewish survivors, I loved them. I transferred my love-hate for Germans to their chilled cousins in mid-Atlantic. What the hell are Germans, after all? Ger-mans are POW's clearing up bombsites, Germans are frigh-tened eyes staring into every newsreel camera from Narvik to Odessa, Germans are the half-mad unshaven mugs of arrested

126

SS men, captured cabinet ministers of the Reich. Reich? This bomb crater on the other side of the Alps. Fuck the Germans, their thousand-year Reich had collapsed after a dozen years. They had had a hostage like me between their fingers and let me go. I had to beat a new enemy, the British and their blockade. And to beat the enemy I had to love and hate him first.

In the camp near Marseilles we slept in tents, queued for food, and made campfires at night. A mixed Boy Scout jamboree. There were plenty of girls in men's shirts and flat-heeled shoes and without makeup. I remembered the type from Gouda. Looked feverishly for a sign of ill-health. But Belsen and Auschwitz must have been holiday camps. There was nothing but a number on their forearms to prove they had ever been to this hell. They all looked pink and well fed, and I couldn't understand why that should be so. In time I found out that most of them had belonged to some Kommando or other, which had special rations. Their task had been to take their relaitves out of the gas chambers and burn them in ovens. I also found one of these pink-cheeked survivors who had consumption, his face was constantly flushed. I felt better.

French- and Greek-chartered boats left Marseilles every week. Certificates were held by people who had held them before the war and were prevented from emigrating by the Germans, and certificates went en bloc to Belsen and Auschwitz survivors who would not or could not go back to their homes in Poland and Hungary. They were the official remnants of the Six Million Dead. I, with my weird story, was not an official survivor and could therefore wait my turn. I wish I had, I might have perfected my French. Instead, I was restless, hanging around for two or three weeks on the Quai observing the procedure of boarding a ship on a collective certificate.

I noticed that names were called up in alphabetical order and what you had to do to identify yourself was to stick up an arm and shout "Here!" First the Asschers and Abrahams, then the Cohens and Hirschmanns, and last the Waschinzkys and Wunschgebildes, and those who were not called up climbed the ropes or had themselves smuggled on board in crates and tarpaulins. The French were glad to see them leave. Even the British immigration officials in Marseilles didn't mind

127

too much how many Jews disappeared in the hold. Only the Jewish Agency, which liked to have a say in the distribution of the visas, was sticky. The comrades of the Agency turned out to be my true enemies.

One Tuesday morning they called Döszö Kemeny, and no loud "Here!" followed within five seconds. I was convinced they were calling me to board the ship. They would have had to search the entire boat to find me, once I was on board. Locked up in a cabin and not ready to leave until we would be far out at sea, I felt as good as under the attic in Retiefstraat, only safer. I just couldn't wait until the boat was finaly moving away from this rat-infested, plagued continent. After two days we made one short stop at Naples, new faces boarded, one man was nearly thrown overboard. The boys from Auschwitz had recognized a block warder and practically lynched him. Block warders were usually inmates themselves. They had to keep discipline in a kennel of starved and half-crazed human animals, which they did with whips and special punishments. The man was arrested by MP's and taken off board. Tempers calmed down.

There were two kinds of people on the boat. Former inmates and others. Nationality didn't matter — yet. What mattered was the number on the right forearm. The numbered and the unnumbered Jews had only this ship in common that carried us all back from where we once, a few thousand years ago, had come. Approaching Haifa, officials of the Agency came on board to lecture us, the illegals (sixteen of us) on the injustice we had done to others who would have to wait now because we had taken their place in the monthly quota. I was a veteran Zionist, Palestine wasn't just any country for me. Palestine was home. For many on the ship it was a bad alternative to New York or Caracas.

Zionism has helped the Jews, anti-Semitism remained a Christian problem. Wherever there were Jews, Jews were hated, driven out, murdered, deported. And all that not since the Cossacks and SS, but as long as history can be told. Hated even in the days of the kings by the surrounding world for their invisible God and peculiar religious laws. Hated even now, though silently, by a large part of the world's population who have to term their anti-Seminitism anti-Zionism to swallow their own deception. Yes, there is a lot wrong with

128

such people or they wouldn't be hated so much. They call it being a Jew. It's just being that's hard, I think.

Now that the Jews of Israel have proved that they can take care of themselves, the situation of Jews has changed. A Jew is no longer someone you have to be sorry for. Jews are tough. They fight well and they win. If there is going to be a next round, and there might be one at any time, they will fight the war in Cairo and Damascus and they will win. And what then? They can take Cairo, Damascus, Beirut and Baghdad. But they can't keep it occupied for long. They will have to go back and wait for the fifth round. Jews can win wars, but they can't move outside the boundaries of the former Palestine. They can gather their tribes back to the Promised Land, but Egypt they were ordered to leave. The Israelis can keep Israel and the world will hate them for it. To be is to be hated, I think.

What a place it must have been two thousand years ago around Easter at a time when He and His disciples, out of their minds on LSD, had thought He wouldn't really die and would get off the Cross at night. They might all have been on drugs. They were certainly high enough to believe they could outsmart monotheistic religion that had functioned well enough with a moral-spiritual message called Jehovah.

He wanted to give a new society of Roman slaves and barbarian pagans a symbol to get this message across in clearer terms. A religious fanatic. A young Jew who wanted to make this world a better place to live in. Rebel with a good cause who ran up against the real-politik of the Establishment. Each of the parties, Pharisees, Sadducees, and Romans, might have used Him for their own political ends, but He was an idealist. His ideal was the betterment of the economic condition for all men, a thing the Jews in their wisdom believed cannot be done in this world but in the next, upon the arrival of the Messiah. All we can do in this world, the Jews believed, is to appeal and remind the builders of idols (from Babylon to Moscow and New York) that idols cannot be worshipped. Material acquisition without social justice will be the doom of every civilization.

Judaism remained a religion — a belief — a hope and prayer. The conscience for all men. *To be* the Messiah is to prepare for the end of the days. Even after two thousand years of Messiah there can be no justice, on the contrary, a successfully expanding population multiplied its greed by multiplying its numbers. Jesus was basically a stupid man, but so are all those who act instead of think and contemplate and move the world at snail's pace with spiritual ideas toward spiritual values. The three kings who came to greet the child Jesus in his crib came from the East of Eden, the representatives of the underdeveloped, backward parts of the world, spokesmen for the underdogs.

The conservative, theocratic Jewish establishment, an embodiment of a wise evolutionary vision, collaborated with the Romans without losing its autonomy. The defenders of Jehovah did not wish to defend Him by going over to aggression. This is not the idea after all. Jehovah had been a warrior until the esoteric club called Jews had conquered its own plot of land. Judaism — a non-aggressive religion — never acquired a nation-state, not until the idea in itself was in peril as its body (the people) were about to be wiped out. The three days sailing from Naples to Haifa (from Rome to Jerusalem) were a magic journey through time and space. I felt I was part of the defeated remnants of an expeditionary force making our way back slowly to an ancestral shrine. As I neared Haifa I thought: Maybe Jesus was right after all, we should have turned Christian and conquered the world by idols and brute force to establish Jewish social justice complete with idols. But if Jesus were right, I prove him wrong now: I am still alive — and my enemy Hitler had to commit suicide. It's either INRI or me. This self has always been Zionist.

Zionism, the gathering of the Exiles, the return of the Lost Tribes, the Rebirth of a Nation, is also rebirth for every single Jew. How to describe this? How to describe love for something as insanely abstract as a country? No amount of skepticism, no degree of laconic gesturing I display now, living here in London in a *normal* time, travelling frequently to various places, can take away this strangely beautiful sensation of 25 July 1945. To see Haifa and the coastline from the deck of the *Askania,* the seeing by itself was seeing the unbelievable. So it hadn't been for nothing and it hadn't been a fantasy. If Palestine exists, so do I. A moment of truth in a specific Jewish neurosis had been reached. Every Jew from anywhere in the world seeing Israel for the first time in his life will testify that the first confrontation with the "country" is an incredible, new, and exciting experience, not to be compared with anything he has ever gone through. The "country" *symbolizes* safety and home.

For the Zionist, Zionism had never been just a political program, it was this as well; above all, it was a kind of psychoanalysis. They call it also a spiritual renaissance. The experience was a near hysteria. Everyone, but literally everyone, either laughed or cried, shouted or talked so loudly, as if the entire ship had been on amphetamine. Everyone on board shared this strange mystical feeling no one could define or wanted to analyze: If this country is *ours*, it is mine privately and personally as well. No non-Jew will ever be able to imagine this weird sensation. He might approximate it by arriving at the home and garden af his ancestors after an escape and long walk from an asylum or jail.

Myself, pretending I didn't care, pretending nothing is worth crying about, forced my tears back and didn't move a muscle. I promised myself an emotional cloudburst at the first sight of Jerusalem. Bypassing His robes, I wanted to look God straight in the eyes. The deception didn't work — I missed my moment of truth. The hysteria turned inward, my stomach didn't like penned-up emotion. When the ship entered the bay and moored, an operation that must have taken at least an hour, I emptied a lifetime of Jewish indigestion and the memory of two thousand years of exile more violently than anyone did on deck with tears streaming from his eyes. I shit on the country of my dreams the first time I saw it because I loved it too much. I was the very last to leave the boat, long after most of the crew had gone ashore. I walked straight down into hundreds of crying faces, all of them so familiar, I thought I knew them by name. All of the tribes of Israel seemed to have gathered to cry for a lost or found relative, to cry away the years of separation or just to cry. On 25 July 1945 the people of Israel were reunited in tears and diarrhoea.

If one of the Palestinians opened his mouth, it sounded like this:

From where are you?

From Holland.

From where are you really?

131

From Vienna.

So you won't know Berl Katzenellenbogen from Lodz?

No.

Berl and my sister Gittel were supposed to be on this boat. Do you have *any idea* why they didn't come?

I don't even know them.

Want to read the letter? He wrote me he is looking for his brother Chaim. Chaim has last been seen alive in Treblinka.

So what's he looking for?

Chaim and his maiden aunt Rivkeh were picked up in Przemysl and were first sent to Baranovitz and up to Kattowitz and from there to Cracow. What a time they must have had. And you? What are you going to do?

I have parents here.

Parents? That's something else. You are a happy man, you have parents. My parents were killed in Radom. Lucky man, he has parents and you are at home in your own country. Be healthy, everything will be all right, you are at home.

I didn't know what the man was talking about. I was a prisoner of the British Mandate Government on my way to the internment camp. If I had parents and two sisters in the country, they must be very busy. I didn't see anyone. I would still have to find them. They seemed to be "at home," not me.

He reappears in an open-necked white shirt and khaki trousers behind barbed wire, wipes his bald head and nose with a handkerchief, is smaller and fatter. He still is my father. Out of breath after ten minutes' walk from the main road to see his son in the detention camp Atlith. Last time I saw my sister she stepped over my head in her nightdress and I saw — for the first time — black hair between legs. Now she wears shorts and a white blouse, is thinner and taller. Her boy friend wears an Australian hat. He is with the Palestine Auxiliary Police Force. They all live in a kibbutz on a mountain not far from the camp I am in. They bring me sweets and cakes, fruit and underwear, and the message that my mother had died. Back in 1941. Of cancer. In a nursing home in Tel Aviv.

The same evening I sleep with a girl called Tamara in a sleeping bag somewhere behind a barracks. What a thrill for two young Zionists to listen to the crickets in the "land of our fathers." My mother is dead. Tamara is alive and moving.

ove you, Tamara; I really love Tamara because my mother died the same day or started living the same day. The place is hot and full of mosquitoes. I sleep in a barracks and can hardly breathe.

From Atlith to Beth Oren in one change by bus. My father helps them with shoe repairs. He has no idea about shoes. His business had been delicatessen, air refreshers for the early cinemas, textiles, foreign exchange, and linen underwear for nuns. But he can't sit around in a kibbutz. Even helping with the repair of shoes leaves him enough time to sit in a chair in front of the small house he lives in and stare into the blue of Haifa Bay. On clear days one can see the top of a mast. The sunken *Patria*. He, my mother, and maybe another three hundred people had made it to the shore. Three hundred and fifty or so were drowned. To prevent the *Patria* from sailing to Mauritius in the wake of the other boats of immigrants, the Haganah had planted a little, but a little too much, TNT in the engine room. The whole ship blew up. The survivors were graciously admitted to the country in spite of the fact that the month's quota was full.

My father stares at the boat and sees the few valuables he had carried with him for a year and a half on a Danube barge, on the bottom of the sea. He whistles through his teeth, breaks a cigarette in half, and smokes the halves in his little wooden cigarette-pipe. This is to curb his smoking. He still smokes eighty halves a day. The heat and the hill are bad for him. He can hardly walk twenty steps without having to gasp for air.

"Why do you smoke so much, Papa?"

"What else have I got to do?" he says.

My eldest sister, it now turns out, is married to the *gafir* — the auxiliary policeman in the Australian hat, a Transylvanian. Sole survivor (later two sisters are found) of eight or eleven children. He has practically walked to Palestine through Turkey and Syria. He works hard in the fields (being a policeman is only a part-time job, to prevent Arabs from getting all the vacancies). He has no profession. He is a good boy. A kibbutznik. "What life is that?" says my father and shrugs. He has been against the marriage and also against his daughter's living with her boy friend without a ceremony. One day they had hauled a rabbi up the mountain from Haifa to marry six couples the same day. But David was working in

133

the orchard at the foot of the mountain, and no one had told
him when the rabbi would arrive, and no one knew exactly
whether he was coming by bus or by lorry. The rabbi couldn'
wait, nor could the other couples, they had to go back to
work. So they married my sister to another man by proxy
Didn't make much difference, but maybe it did. Their mar
riage has never been a happy affair.

The air of the Carmel smells of pines. Beth Oren grow
apples, peaches, and grapes. They work from six in the mor
ning until three. Then they take a shower, have a rest, play
with their children, who spend their days in separate house
where they can sleep as well. The kibbutznik walks slowly
works hard, eats little. With a few exceptions they are al
from Europe. Poland, Czechoslovakia, Russia, Austria, Ger
many. How can they stand the heat and how can they stand
the routine of working, sleeping, eating, and working again
Once in a while they go out singly or together to visit rela
tives or another kibbutz. Their pocket money is about two
pounds a year. Yes, a year. They are *Chaluzim*. The *Chaluz* i
supposed to sing while he works and dance the *Horrah* after
wards. But here they neither dance nor sing, except on holi
days. They are mostly deadbeat and they look sombre. No
surprising. How can they still look at each other, knowing
each other inside out? How can they stand it? Most would
answer: A kibbutz is a kibbutz. It's good for the country
Some will, if pressed, also tell you why a kibbutz is not only
good for the country but also good for its members. Have you
tried finding a job in town? An apartment? Do you have mo
ney? Are you a specialist in some field? And even if you have
all that, remember: This is Palestine, this is not Europe. Jew
must go back to the land. Having been brought up with this
maxim, I had no argument. They are "building the country."

Twenty years later the tents and huts will have changed to
pretty houses. The community dining hall will be panelled
with teakwood. People will have their radios, sewing ma
chines and irons, more pocket money. The good air of the pine
will be for rent to the townspeople, together with a tiled
swimming pool, a view over the sea, and three good meals
day in their holiday resort. They will have a factory and sel
grapes and apples by the ton. It could be foreseen. The *Chalu
zim* are tight-lipped old men with a dream that has come true

their grandchildren play in the supermodern nurseries. They have built the country, and maybe I should have stayed there and helped.

After a few months of watching my father watching the top of a mast of a sunken ship, I decided it was time to leave. For the time being to another kibbutz, because I had no money, no job, no *protectia* and was no specialist. I went to join "friends" from Holland. Every time a new boat arrived in those days after the war, all kinds of people waited on the Quay. The British Police, the Jewish Agency, the Agudath Israel, relatives hoping to find a lost one among the new-comers, and special scouts of various kibbutzim. Some of the kibbutzim offer education, some tempt with beautiful country-side, some seduce with cool, fresh, mountain air, and others offer *chevrah* — a kind of friendship.

"We need you, come to us," the "friends" from Holland said. I didn't want to go to them, nor did I really think they needed me. But after a few months' melancholia under the pine trees I needed them. I needed a different air and went. Galed. I remember a night of rain and storm, waking up in a tent that had fallen on top of us. I remember an afternoon in the fields, loading stones on a cart and watching out for scor-pions. Lifting the stones from the fields was called *ssikool avanim*. The fields were made ready for virgin ploughing and the stones used for building walls. I remember one night, do-ing my turn of night duty, with a real gun across my shoul-der, walking along the barbed wire. Resting in the straw next to the mule and donkey. The donkey knocking an enormous penis against his stomach and screaming for a mate was the only *chaver* who had my understanding and sympathy. In the kitchen, a storm lantern, bread, jam, hot tea, and a couple of chess players. When dawn came up, I was asleep. I was all the time asleep. I still had to catch up with two years in Germany where, I was convinced, I never closed an eye. Those whom I had to wake woke me. Any intruders could have made off with the mule and donkey and the rest of the kibbutz when I was on guard. I didn't care, I was too busy with myself — night and day. At the time the old friends had crossed occu-pied Belgium and France and the Pyrenees together, I'd sailed into Germany on a river barge alone. I was used to going it alone — through I was no longer sure in which direction. Is-rael itself was probably the end of the road, certainly the end

135

of all childish illusions; all I could do with the past insanity was describe it.

Writing was all I thought about. But when was I going to write, what was I going to write and how? I was very tired, I needed a rest. I didn't know where to go, but somewhere where they would let me sleep as long as I like. To want to sleep in Israel is like wanting to sleep in an antheap. There was no place to sleep, unless of course I had family who would support such an outrageous indulgence in the soft life. On the day I arrived someone had told me that I should be happy, because after all I had parents and family. Jews have a mystical reverence for the power of family. I had a father and two sisters in a kibbutz and they wouldn't have minded if I had stretched out there for two years, but the kibbutz would. Rightly so. There was no time for anyone to fall asleep.

It soon emerged that I had also other "family" in the country, all kinds of cousins of my mother. I went to see one, to sample the rest. Solomon Melzer and his wife Grete. Melzer had a shoe repair business and was also a small manufacturer of football boots. He had been "in shoes" even back in Vienna. Our first meeting didn't go off too well. I was neither religious nor intended to become a shoemaker. I was a liability and not an asset. I would cost him money and produce nothing for it. That's all he needed on his doorstep — an eighteen-year-old anarchistic-atheistic, unskilled, and eternally hungry young man in his kitchen and home. He had a better idea. He would take me to Jerusalem to see my uncle Julius Katz, a rich man (Uncle Solomon said) who would help. All I wanted was a bed, aenough bread to live on, to sleep for two full years.

I will take you to Jerusalem, he said, in Jerusalem everything will be all right. Everything better be all right in Jerusalem for a young Zionist, who had sworn a holy oath at the age of eleven and twelve, that he might rather be stricken with a shrinking right arm than forget the Holy City. Was there a better place in the entire world for a Zionist to sleep than at the foot of Mount Zion? Speaking for myself, Uncle Solomon, I am ready to leave for the Moon, I am ready to go back to Europe, to the horror chamber and the fish-eyed spectators

But how would you manage to train my mind to count in inches when I am used to counting in thousands of light years? What difference does an inch of wood, steel, or leather make? But before I go back where I come from, I might as well go first to where I am supposed to have come from. Right down the roots of Jerusalem pines.

Jerusalem talked to me at night with an eerie mystical voice: "Crawl up my womb (it said) and make yourself at home. I am your mother, I am your past, your present, your coffin and your reincarnation. I am your Pyramid and your river. My left breast is the Jordan and my right the Danube. I am the seat of God and the centre of his seat. I am the hole and the memory of Paradise. What you think are clouds are the bulges of my behind. My soft, white buttocks will all be yours. My gate is wide open. Come to me, my lost child, come with all your thrust. Come and sleep with me. Come, jingele, come!"

I had heard this voice all my life. My mother had been the Zionist long before me.

I arrived by bus in the spring of '46, finally, carrying two bags full of football boots from my uncle Solomon Melzer. He had made them for a Jerusalem wholesaler. We arrived on a Friday. The business was settled before Sabbath. After a brief visit to the nearest synagogue, my uncle slept the rest of Saturday, waiting on his bed for the end of the Sabbath and the first bus back. I went for a walk through the Old Town. When I returned at about five, he had in the meantime decided: a) I was a kind of vagabond; b) my unwillingness to become a shoemaker would lead to my ultimate ruin; c) my refusal to join him in his prayers marked me as a heathen; d) Uncle Katz in Jerusalem was probably more suitable and better situated to look after my future. So I shouldn't start this future in Jerusalem entirely broke, he left me one Palestine pound and paid the hotel one night in advance. Then he left. Sunday I went to visit Uncle Katz. A shrewd passerby whom I asked the way warned me: "Julius Katz? Your uncle? He is a wealthy man. You are wasting your time."

He was right. Aunt Selma remembered my "poor good mother" and cried. The uncle was, alas, away on a trip, he would be back the same evening. He would call me at the hotel. Uncle Julius sent a messenger instead, as he was busy. A messenger with a parcel. A gift. A beautifully, hardly visibly

137

mended shirt and a note that said: "Welcome to Jerusalem and good luck." I spent the night in Jerusalem looking for someone to talk to. Home had turned out to be another very cramped town, with some Rich and very many Poor. Just like Vienna. Where the Gruenbergs and Frankels, the Katzes and Silbers live, people we avoided in Vienna. I did not want to stay. Waiting for the bus to Tel Aviv, I turned back into Jan Overbeek on a visit to the Jews. Only more anti-Semitic than most Dutchmen.

Desert is the town; madness is sanity. Things are not what they are, and they are not what they are supposed to be, and they are not what they can be, and they are never what they were. Things are not. Nonethings are indeed hard to describe. And they don't lose gestalt by not being described. Things not described are the gigantic stones, the pyramids, the tombstones along the road. Things that have no name, nameless things, lie on my chest, and I'm not dead yet. Breathing is calling them by their name, speaking is breathing. Breathlessness is the cause of death and I speak for my life. There are, it seems, a lot of people who live quite well without ever saying anything, but what they believe they see, and believe they think, or believe they should say for the sake of communication. They don't speak for their lives like I do. Sadness is with you, Cowboy Moses. The desert is endless, fuck it. How did I get myself in here? I have two thousand miles to go and there are two thousand miles since I left the last outpost of civilization. Two thousand miles from there and two thousand miles from the next place — that gets me somewhere in the middle. I'm neither here nor there. Going up is as painless as going ahead. I might as well go ahead. What more could happen? High-flying B-52's cannot spot me, and even if one would, why should a man up there think there is something wrong with a man who doesn't move? He might think I'm dead and not think about me either. Rescue, I don't believe in it. I think of the old life and of the trail ahead; I even think of making it one day, and what will that be? A short rest, a smoke, a drink, a sleep, then off again. In mid-desert it's good to make accounts. My back burns, my head aches, my tongue sticks to my throat — why did I ever embark on this mad trip? I'm wrestling out of the mud pool, back to the main stream, I'm restless, I want to sail the sea Ulysses has sailed before me. What are they called today, the new men, who go through wars like through a fence? Do we call them cowboys? Where is my memory? I forgot my memory — it's somewhere on a chair in my mother's kitchen. It's an unopened parcel, they will throw it out. And what if they would open it and find my memory? What could they do with it? Would they mail it to me? No one delivers in mid-desert, no one comes here, no one ever comes. It's all in the mind. Cowboy Moses, it's all wrapped up in your mind, memory and all. Shall we unpack, shall we open up, is it time for a late breakfast? No. Not yet. What does it matter? It's something about Middle Europe, it's a long time ago. Why bother? The circumnavigation of Moses the sailor, the flight of the supersonic moonship Moses will go ahead and tear at the wrapping. It will keep me busy. The business of a writer is to talk about this, that, and the other, about the past, about the present, about the future. I'm afraid. I'm afraid the Crucified could, if He wanted to, leave His cross again, climb down and start walking behind me; and I'm also afraid He will not leave the cross, stay up there, and there will be no more resurrection and no more miracles for me. Help! I'm dead! Help!

I write in my diary.

What kind of country is this anyway? I did not like the heat and I did not care for the people. The *chaluz* turned out to be a tight-assed, solid, and stubborn farmer like farmers everywhere else. And the people in town? In Europe all Jews had belonged to the nice, kind, generous, and tolerant species of man. The coarse, rude, hostile, nasty and mean people were "Goyim." But suddenly, wherever you go, a lot of Goyim, claiming to be Jews, thronging the streets. The newcomers, feverish, anxious, and ruthless to get organized, the old immigrants waving you on with the same old tale: "We have been through the same as you. Just wait." If they were kind they would ask, "Have you learned anything? Why did you come here?" I had learnt all the dates of all the Zionist

139

Congresses by heart, two dozen pioneer songs, and ten words of Hebrew, and I had come because Trumpeldor had told me to come. I was also a writer without a language, time, or place to work, but I kept a little notebook with useless reflections:

Misery is not misery. Pain not painful. Nothing hurts. Malcontent is malcontent. What next? What's so special about any one of us? Let's be calm, thankful, and serene, nirvana-minded. Let's think of the three hundred million who are undernourished. Their malcontent lies in your dustbin. Hand them your dustbin. Millions love our dustbin. I hand them my dustbin. Let them choke on the contents. I hate the smell of garbage and paupers. They are everywhere, at any time. The world owes them a dustbin. I know hunger. My mother used to sell old bread to old women who fed it to their chickens. With the money from the old bread my mother bought fresh bread, but we were not allowed to eat it all. Some was left to get old and stale so my mother would have something to sell to buy new fresh bread. Austrian economy '34-'38. We could have remained paupers for life, if Hitler hadn't put an end to it and made us leave (Thank you, Hitler). The rest of the Jews he threw into the flames of God's ever burning love for his chosen people.

I confess to: Escape. Fat Dutch cow-milk (and peanut butter on white sliced) from the Children's Refugee Committee in The Hague drunk straight from the breasts of elderly pious ladies. We were the little Stars of David in the Dutch sky. We lacked the Christian virtues of independence, self-sufficiency, ordinary humanity. I cannot speak for others, but these were my sins: putting their bloody Jesus on the cross, throwing stones at him while he made his way through the narrow streets of Jerusalem. For those sins I was beaten more than once in our street, or maybe, come to think of it, the boys never beat me. I used to be a very fast runner. They should have beaten me. I sinned and was never punished. They should have done to me what I did to their Saviour. Crime deserves punishment. We did it. Yes, we did it. At least I did it, I might as well confess, and the boys didn't beat me because I could run.

140

The punishment was shame. Shame beat us. First in shame and last in maths. The equation of this was simple algebra: Dirt is Dirt. In fact, so dirty was the sky above the Emperor's Mills (our district) not even God's super eyewash could clean our velvet dirty Jewish brown-black-blue eyes. Dirty self-pity was inside the eyes. Self-pity did not help much. But shame is not just poverty, and being Jewish, and a murderer of God's very own son, not just a defiency of vitamins. Shame is also a capital, an asset, not the private property of my family only. In fact, my family had little use for it. shame was the only property shared by most people. It made my personal shame look insignificant: I confess the business of physical survival seemed simple enough. All one had to do is to be careful and lucky. The first twenty years of my life were spent in the business of survival.

Be careful! Don't worry about shame! Be good! We might all die in some apocalyptic disaster. A flood or something of this kind. Be good! means: The space on this earth is very small. without order and justice we cannot expand at the rate we are expanding now. We "Jews" are the sophisticated control room of a five-thousand-foot-high rocket packed with nuclear power. Order and justice for all or we all will die. We are the moralists of this world. The end phase means being two hundred or three hundred years *too early*. The discovery of an America in outer space will come. We are somewhere in the Middle Ages, before a new black plague. Those who survive the plague I don't envy, they will envy you. Our best chance: Let's start the Bomb worship. A new Church. The Cathedral of the Bomb. (They look the same!) The new Christians are the survivors of Hiroshima. Survivors are disciples. I will start this new Church. The fashion in 1975 will be: to look as *maimed* and as *ugly* as possible. Millions of dollars to be earned for the Helena Rubinstein of ugliness. Young men should look like Frankenstein, and the chicks will have plastic surgery to look deformed.

My Chruch of the Bomb. Similar service to cathedral and synagogue. The prayers still have to

141

be written. Maybe we should read a chapter from Freud — on Sunday mornings, indside the Bomb? There is nothing to worship inside one's private mind. We could do that at home. We need gatherings. There is a need for gathering. The idea might catch on gradually — the Bomb stands for a new testament. Where Bomb worshippers are in power, it will soon look like Sweden and Switzerland. Castration promotes wisdom. I would seriously like to talk to someone in Sweden or Switzerland to start the Church of the Holy Bomb.

We lived in a tin hut in a small town called Natanya, where I acquired (the first time in my life) my own table and two chairs, a bed, and a triangle made of wood to hang clothes on. I worked in orange groves, if I could get a day's work. I had a few friends who were fairly amusing. One of them, Edgar Hilsenrath, became a writer. He lives now in New York. I don't know what happened to the others. I was probably the most articulate of the group of friends. I started conversations on literature we didn't read, and art we never saw. The cultural centre of this smal town was the local cinema, showing the leftovers of Hollywood B-films. We were the off-off beat, if anything. Our Mecca was a chair on a terrace in St.-Germain-des-Prés. We were not really articulate in any way, none of us had any education beyond the age of twelve, and held no special political opinions.

Our main topic was how to find a day's work at the local labour exchange. The diet of onions, tomatoes, and oranges got dreary, and the bread at the delicatessen had to be paid for once a week. The rent for the tin hut (we shared with twenty mice) was two days' work. A working day yielded one Palestine pound. Enough to prevent starvation. Dead men hover above all the earthly difficulties; they certainly don't care too much about rents and bills, days of work in the orange groves, or unloading trucks with sand and stones at building sites. I was in a hurry for something to happen but couldn't move. Nor was I going to fight anyone. Of course I loathed the English who fired from behind sandbags on ordinary citizens who were up in rebellion against an unjust Mandate Government and wanted their independence. Of course I loathed the crazy and misguided Arabs who, whipped up by their effendis and adventurists and such old-time Jew-baiters as the Mufti of Jerusalem, cut up busloads full of people coming home from work.

To be on the side of the Jews in the Arab-Israel quarrel, no love for Jews is required. Sympathy for their struggle to survive against bad odds was quite enough. The Jews, whether I liked them or not, are my people, their friends are my friends, and their enemies my enemies. This emotion is easy to produce. More difficult was to stand the sound of explosions. I didn't want to get killed by a bullet; that's why I didn't join any of the various underground armies. To die of hunger, though feasible, would also take a long time. There were still miracles like the odd day of work or a small loan from an acquaintance. Living with papers had been more complicated than living without work. And, anyway, I had to "sacrifice everything" to be a writer one day. And there is no sacrifice without hunger if you like good food.

The Army caught up with my mind I was losing fast, when I had started to work for the telephone company. Our job was to dig holes, erect poles, span wires, lay cables. The Army decided that at twenty-one I was too young for this job but old enough to be taught the Sten gun. I never quite learned how to take this simple gun apart and put it together again. I didn't fire a shot either. Neither blank nor live ammunition. It was difficult enough to run, jump, and march while sound asleep. The MP's who put me in their white puttees soon saw that there was no Military Policeman in me. They sent me to study the secrets of Morse coding and talking through a two-way radio system. I talked to myself most of the time. An air-traffic controller. Me? Whose only Charlie-Baker-Over came from the hollowness of a burnt-out mind. Before this air-traffic adventure I wasted three weeks of Army psychiatrists to let them make out whether I would be "pilot material." How many ways are there to put a simple lock together? The best way is to take yourself time for such a complicated operation. Twenty minutes or so seemed fair to me. I am glad I wasn't present when they read my Rorschach. Maybe I really did only see inkblots. This is what I wrote down, ten times: Inkblot. Every time they showed me a picture I wrote: Inkblot. I wrote Inkblot. Inkblot. Inkblot. Inkblot. Pilots, I'd figured out, must think little and react quickly, they must not show too much fantasy. Therefore: Inkblot when there is one.

143

The last test was an interview. I had mine one wintry afternoon on the third floor of an hotel on the seaside. He was a South African. I forgot his name, alas. He was a nice man, an English gentleman, a pipe smoker, a kindhearted, friendly soul who had immediate understanding and sympathy for my problem of living in the body of one Jan Overbeek under the name of J. L. who was actually J.L. though dead and about to be resurrected in a new body, to leave the old body of J. O with the speed of a Messerschmitt. The Army psychiatrist understood this problem. He smiled benignly. I felt already halfway up the ladder to the cockpit. Why I wanted to be a pilot? What a question! I couldn't say because of privileges accorded to pilots, I couldn't say because of the girls I hoped to meet on my free evenings in Montreal while studying navigation, I couldn't say that I want to be a pilot because I want to be a pilot or because it's marvellous to be a pilot and I love to serve the country. So I said, instead "The pilot, Sir, symbolically crosses the airspace as if it were his own mind in search of the eternal self."

He agreed with my definition, and smiled gently. I gratefully picked up a packet of tobacco that had fallen on the table, spilling some of its contents. I was so happy with my new-won friend, I put a few pictures on the wall right. I confided that I loved *Thus Spake Zarathustra* and could at any time quote passages by heart, and left confident to become the first and only intellectual pilot of the Israeli Air Force, as my South African intellectual friend, too, thought it was about time to help the private intellectual soldier or the Air Force would remain in the hands of peasants and auto mechanics. When I got the news that I could opt for any training in ground personnel but could not be admitted to the pilot school, I was surprised.

I wrote the psychiatrist a note:

"By what means is human consciousness able to modify the tensions of the present so as to have an influence on our events? By no means. The world is not absurd and the mind is surely not incapable of understanding. On the contrary, it may well be that the human mind has already understood the world but doesn't know it yet, or can't say it yet. What do you think?"

He, alas, never replied.

144

Before she came we had had a correspondence so full of loves and kisses and hopes, my last hope now is that this correspondence will never be found. When she arrived, we stayed in bed for six or eight weeks, stayed in bed until we had to start conversation. At this point we didn't know what to say. Yet our living together had to go on. She made me feel that I had made her come to Palestine all the way from Holland. The rest was my responsibility. If anything used to put me off balance, it was the bourgeois word "responsibility." The unattainable and ultimate of all virtues (was not mine). Sentimental by nature, yes, but not responsible. Too much. Let's say I had asked her to come to Palestine because I had wanted a secure sex life and not to leave it to chance. At eighteen it is not easy to get a regular girl unless you are settled or have money. The pleasures she provided increased the guilt. I should have looked for another girl, one without virtues. She was an ordinary, housewifely, quite attractive woman. Good-humoured in general, a bit psychotic. Not bad, but boring. At this time I didn't know this means exactly the same.

She wasn't the kind of woman to travel around with; she wanted to settle down, have children, and be as respectable a housewife as our next-door neighbour. If I wanted to go my own way, I had to divorce her; to divorce her, I had to marry her first. I kept postponing the wedding until I could be sure that I would get the divorce practically the same day. But why did I want to marry to divorce this girl in the first place? Actually, I had no choice. I had lived with her for four years, but only when we talked of separation did she begin to torture me.

Her father would go into mourning because she lives with a man in sin. Orthodox Jews can disown their daughters, and I suppose sons as well, by going into mourning and pretending their child is dead. They tear their clothes (or just undo a stitch on the lapel), put ashes on their head (or wipe their forehead with a rag dipped in ashes), remove their shoes and sit down on a low chair in the middle of the room; occasionally they get up to say the Kaddish, the prayer for the dead. After all that, she would be as dead as if the sea had washed her away. He wouldn't leave her a penny (in his will), not after *her* "death." Nor could the father ever again talk to his child, as she simply didn't exist. What a family! Her parents had never lived happily, as far as she could remember. She

145

didn't get on with her father, disliked him, blamed him, probably wrongly, for her mother's death. She had been very close to her mother. She called her father a primitive man (he had not met him at the time) who had married above his station. The bridegroom was religious and the bride wealthy, a not uncommon combination in Eastern Europe. The rich Jews were, if Orthodox enough, prepared to marry their daughters into another Orthodox family, preferably more *frumm* than themselves, *even* if the bridegroom is not well off, to prove that money is not everything. She was much more cultured (whatever that means) and very attractive and was sold to this narrow-minded, "uncultured" man. Sold to him because of his special good relations with the "Almighty." She was at his mercy. Not surprising that this marriage *à trois* did not work. Her mother had been "a little bit of a mental patient" before the war, and he might not have paid enough attention to her with letters or messages during the years of hiding. Most families were separated at the time, each one sitting it out in his own foxhole, but maybe he hadn't paid her upkeep either?

If one were to investigate a number of private stories, why some people had to die during the war, one might find that some people died because their marriage was dead. A husband glad to get rid of his wife, a wife happy to rid herself of her husband. The Germans were doing the murdering and would ultimately be responsible, they needed less than a helping hand. Mainly to get away from this "Ghetto," a world of pre-1914, from a general nausea with Europe, difficulties of adjustment into an Amsterdam without friends and love, she came to join me. Who can tell? She wanted to get married, if not for her father's sake, for her own. But not at home, where the old man would have arranged the *shiduch* with the help of a marriage broker. I was the bridegroom of her choice.

The answer to a lot of problems was to return to Europe, take her back to her father and say, "Here, Mr. S. Here is your daughter. She is back. Find her a husband." And go on from there to see the world. The father was not poor, he could take care of her. I was ready to leave without any regrets, though afterwards I knew I would feel guilty. Guilty leaving a boat in distress, leaving a burning ship.

Many people who left with me at the time will know this feeling of guilt towards Israel. The war of '48 had been a vic-

146

rious war, I didn't feel that guilty. But I hadn't picked all
e stones, nor erected all the houses, nor planted all the trees
had promised to plant as a child in the Zionist movement. I
ft a lot of stones to be picked by others, trees to be planted
y others, houses to be built by others. There were so many
:ople coming in every day, they would continue where I left
f. I felt very much of an outsider in "my own country,
mong my own people."

The life of the Pioneer, not a bourgeois in the usual sense,
as hardly mine. He was a culture consumer (at its best). The
ms of his culture and its achievements seemed very provin-
al to me. "For the decorations of a dining hall, for this we
eed a painter? Or to write a poem for the next anniversary
f the founding of the kibbutz, for this one needs a poet, *cha-*
er?" The entire "cultural air," like in all small countries, in
l provinces, was to entertain and to decorate only. It was
ot my ambition to settle anyway, and besides, where? Every
wn I visited seemed boring. Why should I live in Haifa all
y life or in Jerusalem? I didn't want to live *anywhere* all my
fe, why go to all this trouble and settle, if you want to leave
ext month maybe? What's so good about the settled life? It's
ernal ennui. But I had a wife to whom I wasn't married,
nd she wanted me to settle. And I might have settled, had some-
ne provided me with a beautiful apartment and insisted,
Now you settle here, I will pay the rent and the upkeep. But
on't move." I waited for this person long enough.

We had no money and that's why Ida was unhappy. Happi-
ess is supposed to be the commodity money *can or cannot*
uy. And that's why we, at home, were a "happy family." We
ad nothing, that's why my father ordered us to give gene-
ously to the man who holds his hand open. The poor man
oes you a favour, not the other way round. The poor man
aakes you feel rich and genrous. "Better to give than to
ake." Yet there was always a strange undercurrent to this
hilosophy of generosity, caused by another's saying "If they
ive to you, take; if they take from you, yell." So with one
and we were generous and with the other greedy. With one
and eighteenth-century aristocrats, and with the other we
lung tenaciously to every bit of possession. No chair was ever
hrown away or it could not "sometimes" be repaired, no
roken coffeemill thrown out or it might be considered first
hether it could not sometimes come in handy.

147

I belonged to the fallen aristocracy about to acquire ba
bourgeois habits. But convinced I am a real better person,
would at the first opportunity clean myself of the love fo
lampshades, mirrors, and bad pictures. Though, as a bette
person, I deserved a better fate than eight hours of rollin
barrels in a warehouse. I also had to make my wife "happy,"
which meant I had to work to buy things. My wife was not
square, she was just an ordinary Jewish girl from an ordinar
Jewish home — she clamoured for security while I wanted n
part of anything in this world. Houses are for burning an
furniture for breaking up. One can live on little food and on
needs no money in the bank. It's fine to eat good food an
nice to have money in the bank, but the aims of this societ
the same as anywhere in the world, are insane.

I loved the aristocrats, the loafers, the hangers-on, th
pretty girls among them, the near artists, dreamers, and in
ventors. Anyone not needing to settle and not willing to settl
was a friend. I felt I was one of them, and yet I wasn't. M
concern was to write. To find time to write. To find either th
kind of job which can provide the time to write, or a chanc
to make enough money ultimately to find time to write. Tim
was the all-important factor. I talked about five lost years an
believed really that years can get lost like handkerchiefs. An
while I loved the arty crowd, I couldn't afford living amongs
them. First of all, I had to make my wife happy. That's why
worked for anyone and for any salary, or nearly anyone.
certainly would not have put up with Sascha Alexander, had
been alone, but maybe I would. I liked to meet those who ha
a long story to tell, because those would be the only peopl
who might also feel obliged to listen to mine.

His father had been a multimillionaire in Baku. Sascha
had burned the money he had escaped with, in the south o
France, on women and film productions. He had arrived i
'32 totally broke ("One big hole in my pocket and nothin
else"), married a blonde from Hamburg called Erika, an
was now the best-known stage photographer in Tel-Aviv. H
was born in a small town in Caucasia, Gurdjieff country, so
of a poor Jewish scrap-metal dealer and a mother who wa
constantly ill. He had five sisters and two brothers. There wa
no money, and the children, between eighteen and eight, wer
mostly left on their own. Father was always away, out "o

148

usiness." (My early sympathy for Sacha was based on the
act that both our fathers had always been away.)

One day a Russian officer of the local garrison asked Alexander, Sr., to come to his house and dismantle an old iron
stove. The officer was a "little cranky." Not only did he not
want any money for the old iron, but he insisted on paying
Alexander to bury the metal, give it a proper funeral, because
"metal has a 'soul' just like a human being," can't be thrown
away. To avoid attracting attention to this somewhat unusual
funeral, they loaded the metal on a cart early one morning
and drove it out to an isolated spot, about fifteen miles out of
town. After the ceremony the officer prayed on the grave of
the metal, and Alexander returned straight home.

After that funeral strange things happened. "He was not
sad, and not melancholic, he was just 'thinking.' He acted
strangely, refused food, but seemed otherwise in good
health.""This twenty-four hours' "thinking" changed the life
and fate of all Alexanders. The old man was convinced that at
exactly the spot they had buried the metal, he would find a
treasure. "I doubt whether he had seen any sign of it while
they were digging the grave — but who knows?" He was convinced that there was not just a bit of oil, but a rich oil well,
right underneath the "grave", with "absolute certainty." He
ould not discuss this mad idea with anyone, least of all the
officer, that's why he was so quiet. But where does a poor,
Jewish scrap-metal dealer get the tools, not to speak of the
money, to buy the land and drill for oil? There was only one
solution — he had to come to some sort of an agreement with
the owners of the land.

One night when everyone had gone to sleep, he sat alone at
the table, stared at the flame of the kerosene lamp and
"thought." He, who could neither read nor write, took a piece
of paper and a pencil and started to draw. A map one couldn't
really call it. On the top half of the paper he drew trees,
bushes, grass, and a rabbit, and on the lower half something
that looked like a mountain or palm tree. The oil well.

The next morning the old man was gone. As some of his
clothing was gone too, everyone was convinced that he had
just lost his mind and disappeared. He must have left in the
middle of the night. Not even the neighbours had heard him
leave. He was gone four or five months. One night he returned as suddenly as he had left. When he arrived, half the

town woke up. He came in a chauffeur-driven automobil
dressed in the latest fashion. A rich man. "From the poore
of the poor we became the richest of the rich." All because
this absolute certainty.

Sascha Alexander, whose father had struck it rich by "c
incidence," believed with "absolute certainty" that phot
graphy is magic and has nothing to do with light cells a
chemicals. He experimented with a developer to be taken i
ternally with a spoon like medicine: "The aim of photograp
cannot be the objective but only the subjective image of t
viewer. No need everyone should see the same thing. If peop
would drink some of my special developer (which still has
be invented), they can see whatever they like, providing th
know the exact time of exposure to their eyes!" (You are
writer, he said, there is a book for you here.)

Sascha Alexander inspired me. There was something abo
this man, his weird background and insane views that start
me on my own quest to find the right exposure for my ow
magic negative. In myself, too, I found images yet undev
oped, in need of a certain amount of chemical rearrangeme
to make the invisible become real. Writing, it struck me, is
kind of photochemical process. It is a matter of right propo
tions applied in a correct way before I could obtain co
vincing positive results. The father buries the metals a
unearths a well of material riches, the son does the same
another more mechanical dimension of his mind.

In the unending chain of fathers and sons, masters a
pupils I was ready to learn, or rather willing to learn a lesso
Slowly, while apparently busy writing numbers and letters c
narrow sides of folders, I grasped the essence of my own re
lity as a mixture of inner and outer experiences. If fear
men and destruction of all men's material values, includi
his very physical existence, had contributed to my apparent
accidental survival, I myself had been on this flight into a
other infinite dimension since my very first days I entered th
world, accelerating the speed in which I travelled in the se
onds between life and death during the war years. And th
rocket was gathering momentum merely because it continu
on its path. The philosophical problem of linear or circul
concept of all things alive was hardly mine: I still exist
therefore I move ahead, and because I am alive, I can go c
living forever. If life is never ending, man's labour is not req

ed to sustain only to improve the condition of his existence.
o make visible what is not and positive what is negative is
ndergoing a photochemical process consciously. To know, to
e aware is to move — *ergo sum,* I discovered by reflecting a
urned-out, basically tired mind on Sascha Alexander's idea
 swallow developer in order to see images. The sanest thing
nyone ever suggested. There was no drug and no such deve-
•per around in Tel-Aviv in late 1949, only this one eccentric
ussian photographer to soak my brain with the suggestion of
chemical, not with the chemical itself.

Fantasy can turn any real experience into the acceptance
f its reality. If I could tell on paper, black and white, of
very single one of my previous deaths it would certainly be a
od beginning to consider one day, at some later stage of
emical development, the position of others. For the time
eing I had to shed oceans of tears for something irreversible,
ke the death of my Jewish world, before I could wipe my face
ith sarcasm towards the recent past. I called it *The Diary of
anan Edgar Malinek,* claimed that I had found it half bu-
ed in Negev sand after one of the fiercest battles in the war
f independence of 1948/49, the battle of Iraqu el Sudein. I
yself had never seen south of Jerusalem and the most time
f the war I'd spend in a Tel-Aviv hotel room or drinking
offee on an open terrace overlooking happily playing sunbat-
ers on the beach.

Hanan Edgar Malinek, a young man of nineteen, had just
rrived in the country after years of concentration camps and
vo years postwar refugee camp in Germany, straight from
e boat. He is driven to a camp where he is taught within two
eeks the handling of Bren and Sten gun and the use of
andgrenades, is transported to the front and into the heat of
attle, and is dead in less than four weeks. The death he had
urvived in Belsen was not in Belsen but in us, the nation of
nbathers. On the one hand I mourned Malinek's death sen-
mentally; on the other I agreed it had to happen just like
at. The sunbathers on the beach had to go on playing their
ames, we can't all die, nor can we forget that some do. As
alinek, like so many thousands of survivors, had lost all
elatives in Europe to mourn him (one of the reasons why
oung newcomers were packed off to the front upon arrival
as that no one would ever know or miss them if they disap-
eared), *The Diary* was my private monument for the

151

invisible soldier in myself, lamenting the loss of my courag
celebrating unconscious heroism as a freakish mistake
nature called temporary existence.

"Why, if I am born, am I not born forever?" Malinek as
in his diary, knowing he will never get out alive from t
trenches around the police fortress in the Negev. I buried hi
with a mad ritual (in this instance, a Kaddish read by some
his comrades), a prayer for the death of men and metal
through which a Russian officer in Baku had found peace
his soul and a Jewish scrap merchant (skeptical as Jews are
the wealth of superabundance. I myself made thirty Palestin
pounds for six instalments, enough to convince me that wri
ing *all writing*, is a bit of merchandise, a pleasantly wrappe
up household gadget from the moment a merchant of printe
paper (also called publisher) gets hold of it.

The Diary of Hanan Edgar Malinek helped to develo
something else in the chemistry of my mind: I realized that
had been, all along, afraid of the financial award that com
with publication and exposure of hidden pains. Sascha Ale
ander, the photographer, taught me how to use my eyesigh
my vision, and how vision convincingly expressed creat
monetary by-products, inseparable from one another as pos
tive from negative.

After Sascha Alexander, for whom I carried lamps an
cameras to the theatre, for five pounds a week (which he n
ver paid), I became three things at once. Writer, actor an
civil servant. At night I shaved Yossef Jadin, the lead in *Bor
Yesterday*, or stood on the stage of the Cameri Theatre in
pink uniform, watching the audience as the audience watche
me as a soldier in Ivgenye Schwartz's *The Shadow*. By day
continued to scribble numbers and letters on the narrow sid
of folders. The writing on the front of folders wasn't diff
cult, there was plenty of space; the writing on the side was
headache. Entire numbers and letters got lost. Yet, because
was a writer, the author of *The Diary of Hanan Edgar Mal
nek*, people in the office were nice to me. The entire offic
had read each of the instalments of *The Diary* (it had a
peared in a weekly called *Ashmoret*). They were honoure
to work with "a real artist" in the room.

This monster of a sentimental fake diary saved my nec
The government for a while let me write numbers and lette

152

on files for a modest few pounds a week, but was not going to feed me for the rest of my life. I would have to produce diaries of the same kind every month, but I had absolutely no idea what would sell. Besides, I disliked the language I wrote in; I hated German, the language I knew best. I couldn't stand the sound of it. I needed a new language to express feelings and ideas I hardly knew how to formulate. The heroic frown of the anarchist rebel did not suit me, the catatonic expression of the Marxist-Leninist mind was wrong, the guilty look of the Western democrat I did not like on my face, it's alien to me, the esoteric stare into the next world of my Buddhist self frightened me, the laughter of Zen turns into a grimace, and the resigned eyes of the pious are not mine. I myself was happy just with peace and wanting nothing but peace, and as there was now peace in Europe, and I had had my five years of sleep, I could face the rats of this plague-stricken continent again.

War

☐ **James Clavell**   **KING RAT**   **40p**
Rat-like humans in a notorious Japanese POW camp. King Rat
is an every-man-for-himself US sergeant who lives high at the
expense of others – and finally pays the brutal price.

☐ **Hugh Wray McCann**   **UTMOST FISH**   **30p**
A *very* odd episode from world war one. Equatorial East Africa,
well-officered, highly professional German troops, and against them
a handful of green Britishers. Result – not what you might think.

☐ **David Forrest**   **THE LAST BLUE SEA**   **25p**
The second world war – the Australian Expeditionary Force
(amateur soldiers if ever there were) against the hair-trigger-trained
Japanese in tropical, unexplored Papua.

☐ **Gore Vidal**   **WILLIWAW**   **25p**
US naval war in the Arctic. The Japs are bad enough, but then
Nature takes a murderous hand in the game. The pace never lets
up. By the author – surprisingly! – of MYRA BRECKINRIDGE.

☐ **Ray Rigby**   **JACKSON'S WAR**   **35p**
A war like no other; skilfully waged by 'NAAFI troops' hundreds
of miles behind the 8th Army battle line. 'Permissiveness' may well
have hilariously begun here.

☐ **J. P. W. Mallalieu**   **VERY ORDINARY
SEAMAN**   **25p**
By a writer who was there – life below decks on the high seas
during the last war. Many grim moments, but the ability of the
common seamen – most of them 'civilians in uniform' – to forge a
warmly human world in their stark, confined quarters makes this
one of the most triumphant books ever published.

People

☐ **Robert Tressell**   **THE RAGGED-TROUSER-ED PHILANTHROPISTS**

50p

The miserable reality of working class life during the Edwardian Golden Age. The first English socialist novel and as passionately alive – and relevant – as ever.

☐ **George Eliot**   **FELIX HOLT THE RADICAL**   **40p**

From the great period of English novels, the story of conflict between a noble-minded young reformer and a typical 'corrupt for the best reasons' Victorian politician, and of the heroine Esther, torn between them both.

☐ **Arthur Morrison**   **A CHILD OF THE JAGO**   **35p**

A masterpiece of social fiction set in the boisterous, brawling East End of last century's London. H. G. Wells reviewed it on publication and praised it highly. The author is the nearest we have to an English Zola, and by no means suffers in the comparison.

☐ **Edward Blishen**   **THIS RIGHT SOFT LOT**   **30p**

A 'Blackboard Jungle', London style: a secondary modern where most of the pupils have abandoned lessons in favour of fisticuffs, thieving and girls. Most of the teachers have given up. But one of them is convinced that the kids are *not* beyond hope. 'There isn't a dull page' – *Sunday Mirror*

☐ **Krupskaya**   **MEMORIES OF LENIN 40p**

Lenin's shadow looms immense 47 years after his death. Millions of words have been written about him – but never anything as intimate as this moving book by his widow and lifelong companion. 'A portrait of a great and honest man' – Arnold Bennett, *Evening Standard*

☐ **James Agee and Walker Evans**   **LET US NOW PRAISE FAMOUS MEN**   **75p**

One of the most famous of all twentieth century books. The 'poor whites' of the American Deep South during the Depression of the 1930's. Agee and Evans, his photographer, were sent there on a journalistic assignment, and the rare result is this masterpiece account.
'Magnificent and convincing, because Agee's involvement is so complete' – *The Guardian*

Some Continentals

☐ **Roger Peyrefitte**   **THE JEWS**   **50p**
Lovely Osmonde shocks her family because she wants to marry a
Jew – but as the witty author scarifyingly shows: if she can't marry
someone with Jewish blood . . . there may well be no-one left she
can marry.

☐ **Robert Musil**   **YOUNG TORLESS**   **30p**
A homosexual novel from one of Europe's great modern writers
about four cadets enmeshed in the machinery of a Teutonic military
academy. The systematic bullying that only too often degenerates
into torture is horrifying reading. 'I strongly recommend it' – *Punch*

☐ **Jean-Paul Sartre**   **INTIMACY**   **30p**
Ranges over the whole field of today's arid spirituality, from the
anguished conflict between 'love' and 'sex' to the feverish childhood
of a fascist rabble-rouser-to-be. A key book to modern life.

☐ **Agnar Mykle**   **LASSO ROUND
THE MOON**   **30p**
The multi-million-selling novel of Scandinavian youth and sex.

☐ **Alberto Moravia**   **COMMAND AND I
WILL OBEY YOU**   **30p**
Twenty-seven short-short razor-sharp stories by the world-famous
author of THE WOMAN OF ROME. 'One of the greatest living
writers, and this volume is a harsh, pungent, delicious pleasure' –
New Statesman

☐ **Hermann Hesse**   **DEMIAN**   **30p**
Hesse has become a modern 'cult' figure. DEMIAN, eerily mystical,
deals with the progress of a confused young man to some sort of
final enlightment – which is achieved on a hallucinatory World
War I battlefield in the novel's climactic last chapter. DEMIAN is
already in its fourth Panther Books edition.

Not Only for Students . . .

☐ **Chaucer (in modern prose by David Wright)**   **THE CANTERBURY TALES**   40p

The best version available. 'In Mr. Wright's modern English the tales become pure story-telling without losing the flavour of the oldest of English writers' – *The Bookman*. And *Tribune* adds: 'Mr. Wright can be as coarse as Chaucer'.

☐ **(translated by David Wright)**   **BEOWULF**   25p

Our only epic poem, and perhaps the earliest considerable poem in any modern language; it brings the doom-laden society of 6th century Anglo-Saxondom to glowing life. Wright's translation surpasses even William Morris's.

☐ **Frederick Engels**   **THE CONDITION OF THE WORKING CLASS IN ENGLAND**   40p

The modern world in all its facets was born 150 years ago in England. This is the classic account of that harsh birth.

☐ **D. E. Jones**   **INTRODUCTION TO PSYCHOLOGY**   50p

'This is the best introductory text I have read – simple terms and simple sentence construction, supported by examples from everyday life. If you are new to the field, here is your first book' – *Housecraft*

☐ **J. W. B. Douglas**   **THE HOME AND THE SCHOOL**   40p

Dr. Douglas's famous study of 5,000 boys and girls through their primary school years is essential reading for teachers and parents and all who are concerned with education. The conclusion begins to emerge that the success of a child's school career is much more connected with his home background, his social background, than it is with his original brightness.

☐ **J. W. B. Douglas and others**   **ALL OUR FUTURE**   40p

This important sequel to THE HOME AND THE SCHOOL takes the study of the 5,000 boys and girls from their eleventh to their fifteenth years, and the earlier book's suggestion – that not so much intelligence but social background ensures academic success – is reinforced. Both books have been recommended as basic reading by Unesco's *Bulletin of the International Bureau of Education*

Today's World

☐ **Eldridge Cleaver**   **SOUL ON ICE**   **30p**
White racial myths, sex between blacks and whites, black freedom
in the U.S., and many other explosive topics, in a series of open
letters by a Black Panther leader (now living in exile in Algiers)
written while he was serving nine years in Folsom Prison,
California. 'Essential reading' – *New Statesman*

☐ **Eldridge Cleaver**   **POST-PRISON**
                                WRITINGS AND
                                SPEECHES   **40p**
Key book by America's most famous black revolutionary.
'Essential addendum to SOUL ON ICE. As powerfully seductive
as anything being written anywhere in the world . . . piercing,
brilliantly oratorical, poisonously funny, quotable until the cows
come home' – *New Society*. 'After reading Cleaver we cannot say
we do not know what the struggle is about' – *Spectator*

☐ **Nicholas Deakin**   **COLOUR, CITIZENSHIP**
                               AND BRITISH
                               SOCIETY   **50p**
Abridged and updated edition of the famous Institute of Race
Relations report, *Colour and Citizenship*. With the publication of
this book no one has any longer any excuse for not knowing what
the real situation is. 'Will certainly become a classic standard work
on colour and race relations in Britain' – *Sunday Telegraph*

☐ **Ann Cornelisen**   **TORREGRECA**   **50p**
A study of life in a modern Italian village – modern? Read this
shocking account and you're back in medieval Europe's dark ages.
'A documentary of human beings in adversity – it deserves a place
next to Oscar Lewis's CHILDREN OF SANCHEZ' – *Time*
Magazine

☐ **R. W. Reid**   **TONGUES OF**
                          CONSCIENCE   **50p**
Sub-titled 'War and the Scientist's Dilemma', this book is a
searching inquiry into the scientist's responsibility for the vile use
that his discoveries are often put to. Its conclusion: the scientist
should become more aware – but *so also should the man-in-the-
street.*

☐ **Anthony Sampson**   **THE NEW**
                               EUROPEANS   **50p**
Topical if ever a book was. A cool look at Common Market Europe
at work and at play, all the way down from the biggest of big
business to the unskilled working man. Food and food
prices, housing and rents, in health and in sickness – it's all here.
'Seems likely to remain a classic' – *Wall Street Journal*

Highly-Praised Modern Novels

☐ **John Fowles**   **THE FRENCH**
                                     LIEUTENANT'S
                                     WOMAN   40p

Although Fowles is an English – and *how* – writer his novel has
been on the American bestseller lists for months. To read it is an
experience. 'When the book's one sexual encounter takes place it's so
explosive it nearly blows the top of your head off' – *New York
Saturday Review*

☐ **David Caute**   **THE DECLINE OF**
                                     THE WEST   50p

A newly independent African state in bloody turmoil, and the
world's adventurers – male and female – home in like vultures.
Strong reading.

☐ **John Barth**   **THE SOT-WEED**
                                     FACTOR   75p

The story of a mid-eighteenth century man of fortune, told in a
modern spirit by one of America's great writers. 'Most magnificent,
totally scandalous' – Patrick Campbell, *The Sunday Times*

☐ **Elizabeth Bowen**   **EVA TROUT**   35p
'Elizabeth Bowen is a splendid artist, intelligent, generous and
acutely aware, who has been telling her readers for years that love
is a necessity, and that its loss or absence is the greatest tragedy
man knows' – *Financial Times*

☐ **Norman Mailer**   **THE NAKED AND**
                                     THE DEAD   60p

The greatest novel from world war two.

☐ **Mordecai Richler**   **COCKSURE**   35p
Constantly reprinted by public demand. The brilliant satiric picture
of a tycoon whose business and sexual appetites know no limits.

Obtainable from all booksellers and newsagents. If you have
any difficulty please send purchase price plus 5p postage per
book to Panther Cash Sales, P.O. Box 11, Falmouth, Cornwall.

I enclose a cheque/postal order for titles ticked above plus 5p.
a book to cover postage and packing.

Name _____

Address _____
